The Business Planning Tool Kit

A workbook for
the primary care team

Independent Health Advisor
Management Consultant to General Practice

fe Medical Press

Radcliffe Medical Press Ltd
18 Marcham Road
Abingdon
Oxon OX14 1AA
United Kingdom

www.radcliffe-oxford.com
The Radcliffe Medical Press electronic catalogue and online ordering facility.
Direct sales to anywhere in the world.

———————————————

British Library Cataloguing in Publication Data

A catalogue record for this book is available from the British Library.

ISBN 1 85775 500 6

Typeset by Advance Typesetting Ltd, Oxfordshire
Printed and bound by TJ International Ltd, Padstow, Cornwall

Contents

Foreword

Primary care has moved on from the days when a practice was run by the partners at a monthly meeting, with a manager, promoted from receptionist, attending to the paperwork. The legacy of those days is, however, still with us. As organisations, practices are more often found reacting painfully to the demands made on them rather than moving forward according to a strategic plan. Two considerations alone are sufficient to explain this: the employers are clinicians with no training and often little interest in management; and general practice is one of the few businesses where providing a better quality service is more likely to lead to financial loss than gain.

This book provides a whole new way of looking at how general practice can be managed and it does so in the form of a manual which gives whoever takes on the task the tools to do so. It is based on the philosophy that a successful business is not one that focuses on increasing profits but one that attends to the health of the organisation and especially to the people working in it.

The book starts with a practical guide on how a practice can draw up a business plan. The rest of the book is about what should be in that plan and how to achieve it. This is a concept of a business plan in its widest sense: it encompasses clinical governance, dealing with risk management, performance assessment, how to incorporate NHS priorities, revalidation, Personal Learning Plans and Practice Professional Development Plans, and how to obtain feedback from patients about the service they are receiving. Some chapters deal with practical issues: prescribing, audit, appraisals, training and employment law. Other chapters tackle less tangible issues, managing change or communication, but always with a practical slant, even down to a guide on how to be a whistleblower.

This is not a comprehensive guide to practice management. It does not give a comprehensive account, for instance, of employment law or how to implement a National Service Framework. What it does is to describe, in detail, how a practice can set about the business of managing itself well. The whole book is shot through with the belief that the processes described are not 'add-ons' but essential ingredients of the way the practice functions.

The layout of the book is a joy. Every section has space in which staff members can write their comments on the issue in hand. Indeed, the involvement of every member of staff in the management process is another consistent theme of the book. As Annie Phillips quotes Tony Benn as saying:

'Discussion is the most radical thing in the world, which is why no system ever wants you to talk about anything. They don't want you to get together and come to a conclusion because it may not be the kind of conclusion they like.'

Users of this book will find that strategic management takes an awful lot of time and may involve conclusions they don't like, but they are likely to find themselves in a healthier practice because of it.

Andrew Polmear FRCP FRCGP
Senior Research Fellow
Academic Unit of Primary Care
The Trafford Centre
University of Sussex
December 2001

About the author

Annie Phillips has written professionally about health and health management since she qualified as a speech and language therapist in 1978. She has over 20 years' NHS experience in primary and secondary care as a clinician and manager.

Her 10 years as a speech and language therapist led to the research and publication of an international dysphasia/dementia screening test, presented at the 1986 British Aphasiology Conference. She has won various prizes and awards for her subsequent work, and in the 1990s she was a finalist in *Medeconomics'* Good Management Awards, and regional winner in a national British Institute of Management competition on change management.

She worked as a practice and fund manager for a five-partner training practice in central Brighton from 1989 to 1998; from then as an independent health advisor, trainer, and management consultant to general practice, PCG/Ts and health authorities.

Throughout her career she has written extensively for the therapy, GP and management press. She currently writes on contemporary management issues for a range of publications, including the *Health Service Journal*, *Community Care*, *Doctor*, *Primary Care Manager* and Croner Publications, with a focus on healthcare politics and human resource management.

As a management consultant, her interest is in organisational analysis and the development of healthy organisations, with a focus on finding ways to manage stresses and conflicts, understanding and alleviating dysfunctional communication and developing effective management strategies.

Annie can be contacted via aphillips@cwcom.net or www.anniephillips.co.uk.

The website

There is a website to accompany this book and this can be found at:

www.radcliffe-oxford.com/busplan

The site includes additional resources, e.g. examples, templates and guidelines, as referred to throughout the main text of the book.

Acknowledgements

My very special thanks go to Lin, my partner, and my son Chris, who have tirelessly supported, sustained and encouraged me throughout the writing process.

Particular thanks to my colleagues at the Ouse Valley PCG, ESBHHA, and the MAAG, for providing me with valued information on current working practice. Also to Laurie Mullins, Associate Principal Lecturer at the Business School, University of Portsmouth, whose 5th edition of *Management and Organisational Behaviour* (Pitman Publishing, 1999) was the inspiration behind the information on organisational structure and performance.

Special thanks to Andrew Polmear for agreeing to write the foreword; and the number of people who may be unaware how much their friendship, support and interest in this project have, in a variety of ways, helped in its completion, including, amongst others too numerous to mention, Denise Rendell, Anne Cross and Fiona Bilton.

I also wish to record my thanks and debt of gratitude to all staff and partners – especially Dr Howard Carter – for the help, support and valuable advice gained during my employment at St Peter's Medical Centre, Brighton, 1989–98. Without them this book would not have been possible.

Finally, I want to thank all those whose thoughts and ideas have, over the years, found their way into my subconscious, so that they are now indistinguishable from my own. I have given references for sources of work by other writers but apologise to any concerned if acknowledgement has inadvertently not been recorded. Should you note any queries, errors or omissions, please contact the publisher.

Annie Phillips
December 2001

PART ONE

CHAPTER 1

Why business plan?

Introduction

The NHS Act (1999) offers practices new opportunities to develop their business. By April 2002 it is expected that nearly a third of GPs will be working to a PMS contract: practices will be expected to develop and write business plans, and all practices will now be encouraged to write Practice Professional Development Plans (PPDPs). This interactive workbook has been written with all members of the primary healthcare team in mind – for busy GPs and primary care/practice managers in particular. It aims to guide practices step by step through the process of business planning.

It is not just PMS practices that will benefit from business planning but any practice that is:

- rapidly developing or overloaded
- noting big problems that prevent full-capacity working
- feeling overwhelmed or out of control.

Successful businesses do not focus on maximising profits but minimising losses. This book tells you how to do this by covering all aspects of practice business planning and organisational analysis: the service, finances, premises, the skills of your team.

This workbook looks at the issues you need to consider before embarking on, or developing, your business in general practice. Its aim is to guide the busy practice through the process of business planning. Whatever stage your business is at – your practice may have been established for many years, or you may be considering moving to new premises – it is essential to consider all aspects of the business. In collectively thinking about, then writing the business plan, the practice grounds itself as a business and sets the footings down to grow and broaden and develop in the healthcare business. Practices that are rapidly developing, overloaded, or looking to take up the latest government offers of a Personal Medical Services Contract would find this process invaluable.

This is a book not just for entrepreneurs, self-starters or the opportunist, but it will help if you see yourself as one of these. It is designed for those who want to see their practice not just as a successful business, but as a flourishing one. It is also aimed at those of you who have big problems to solve within the practice; problems that prevent you and others in the team from working to their full capacity. You may feel overwhelmed by events out of your control, or simply feel the business has grown to a point where you no longer feel you are in control. Both the ambitious and cautious will benefit from business planning.

The introduction of continuing professional development (CPD) for all workers in the NHS[1] will encompass the entire workforce, so effective business planning will be essential. The process will need to reflect the global picture, accounting for:

- national service frameworks
- clinical governance initiatives
- national and local priorities.

You need to know:

- how you are doing
- where you are now
- where you want to go
- how you get there.

This clarity is essential to enable personal development plans and learning needs to be linked to outcomes.

The NHS Act 1999 has set new standards, one of which is the Improving Working Lives (IWL) Standard. This means that every member of staff working within the NHS is entitled to belong to an organisation which can prove it is investing in training and development. One of the key objectives is for organisations to conduct annual attitude surveys – asking relevant questions and acting on the key messages. This book shows you how.

This book is designed as an interactive workbook. The reader can complete it, but it will work best if used as a training tool. One person's view is fine, but to have the whole practice input will be immeasurably useful. Also, one person, however senior in the practice, will not be able to carry through all the changes on her/his own. Big change needs to be understood and owned, not imposed. So use the opportunity to have an away day, or have a series of practice meetings, to look at your business now, and how you want it to be.

Make this book work for you. Dip into it, read it from beginning to end, do the exercises alone to begin with then photocopy relevant bits as questionnaires for the rest of the practice team. I have marked these exercises to assist you.

> ⇒ **For the nurses**
>
> ⇒ **For the doctors and manager**
>
> ⇒ **For the staff**
>
> ⇒ **For the whole team**

I have marked common problems and their solutions with

- I have used this bullet point for information only
- ○ and this one when there is a question for you.

In this first section, we look at some of the thinking behind business planning, and begin to examine what to include in the business plan for your practice. The planning process is important. If, after completing this book, you do not choose to formally write a business plan, the collective effort involving all the practice team is an education in itself. Without such planning, ideas and visions are woolly and impractical, especially if unshared or not agreed by all parties.

However, if you do produce a document it will give you a solid foundation from which to launch your new ideas – these are more likely to succeed if shared, owned and understood by everybody. Normally, prior to launching a business, the prospective entrepreneur would write a business plan to be issued to their professional advisors. In general practice, of course, this is not the case. Most practitioners start with the assumption that their business cannot fail, and indeed, it is unlikely to. We will always need doctors, and while we have an NHS, doctors have a guaranteed job for life. However, life is full of change, and the cautious GP will be one that can plan ahead and adapt to that change, preferably in advance of it happening. The practice will then be in control of events rather than simply responding. A business plan enables the practice to take a *strategic* view of events, rather than being *reactive*.

Reactive management is crisis ridden, *proactive* planning is good for:

- time management
- personal organisation
- organisational development
- aiding clarity and vision.

Any organisation that plans ahead considers different levels of strategy:

- operational (meetings, etc.)
- tactical (a look at next month, a review of the quarterly returns)
- strategic (a 3–5 year plan).

Which level is your practice good at?

When forward planning, practices need to bear in mind the forces that impact on their organisation:

- economic trends
- demographic trends
- sociological forces
- psychological forces
- legal influences
- governmental influences
- technological developments.

General practice does not run in a vacuum. Consider the impact on your practice if the elderly population increases substantially, the poverty that causes ill-health rises, or new drugs cure cancer altogether. A business plan helps practices address the impact of some of these issues, and gives practices the tools to change to meet the challenges ahead.

The business plan discussed here could still be issued to all the practice's professional advisors: the bank manager and the accountant. The practice may not prefer to issue a copy to their PCG/T but may wish to select portions for issue. Most practices keep information about practice income and expenditure private to the practice and its own business associates. Sharing the plan helps clarify some of the wider issues, and helps firm up the proposals so that all involved can see whether the business plans are going to be viable or not. It is also useful to see if the practice's own business plans tie in with those of other local and national groups – business and political. This could be one of the first questions to ask yourself.

$\Longrightarrow$ **For the whole team**

Do the practice aims and objectives coincide with those of the NHS as a whole?

- Value for money.
- Better services.
- Improving health.
- Effective organisation.

To summarise, the process of planning the future of the business enables the practice to:

- see clearly where they are at present
- clarify some of the wider issues facing the business
- firm up any new proposals
- evaluate the practice and its patients, detailing the strengths and weaknesses
- provide a statement of intent for interested stakeholders
- formulate goals
- identify the action needed to achieve these goals
- identify resources required in terms of skills, activity and finance
- anticipate and plan for problems
- ensure the negotiation of the best possible funding.

  For the whole team

How do we plan?

- Identify the problem.
- Collect the data to quantify the problem.
- Analyse the problem.
- Organise and co-ordinate a plan of action.
- Implement.
- Review.
- Monitor.

Sounds suspiciously like the audit cycle doesn't it?

Good planning involves:

- objectivity
- realism
- flexibility
- logical thinking
- wide communication
- everyone's involvement
- delegation
- team work
- time.

Have you got this in your team?

When formulating a business plan we need to look at the following:[2]

- practice aims and objectives
- partnership structure
- current and future patient services
- the list size
- outside commitments
- the building and equipment
- clinical performance
- finance
- overall strengths and weaknesses
- external forces that may impact on the practice future.

In this first chapter we look at some recommendations for surveying your practice.

How do we collect the information we need?

There is work to do. There are many ways the information you need can be collected:

- through individual interviews with key practice members
- through questionnaires issued to the whole practice
- through a series of meetings where the main headings are presented for discussion.

As time is often at a premium, one of the quickest ways is to issue questionnaires then back this up with a series of follow up meetings when the collected and collated ideas are re-distributed and presented back for discussion.

Survey the health of your organisation

Questionnaires should be:

- fun
- easy
- creative
- innovative.

The questions should:

- be wide ranging
- elicit a *feel* for the issues
- ask what motivates
- ask about the main practice strengths and weaknesses
- encourage honesty
- be anonymous.

They should be fun to produce, complete and analyse. If you are creative, this will encourage innovation and creativity within the practice. The questions could be wide ranging to enable you to elicit a feel for the issues that are dear to people's hearts – what motivates the staff and partners, what people feel are the main practice strengths and weaknesses. They should encourage honesty: people may prefer anonymity; the feedback should be anonymous at least.

 For the facilitator

Some of the questions will provoke strong feelings, and you will need to give space for these to be aired. Don't expect to bury a can of worms! If you are working this through in a team, expect tensions, arguments and difficulties. Everyone will have a different agenda.

- Feelings often produce more creative solutions to problems.
- Being there can be enough, you do not have to solve the problem.
- Empathise so the problem is shared.
- Create a safe, confidential space to air any conflicts.
- Prioritise doubts and uncertainties.
- Allow and encourage conflict.
- Tolerate criticism directed at you.
- Support those less socially skilled.
- Learning is best achieved by honest sharing.
- Be prepared to take risks.

Some of the questions in the following questionnaires are based on a Soft Systems Approach, developed by Peter Checkland in *Systems Thinking, Systems Practice*.[3] This was developed as an approach to problem solving in an organisation, and helps both to identify and analyse problems which are in complex and confusing settings – like general practice.

You may identify some of the problems as 'messes'. These may feel unmanageable, impossible to untangle, unsolvable, and tend not to have clear boundaries. Other types of problem identified through this approach may just be 'difficulties': smaller, with fewer people involved, with limited implications and likely solutions known. These may be treated separately, with clearer priority.

Use brainstorming where possible. Brainstorming:

- involves everyone
- is non-threatening
- encourages communication and creativity
- maximises solutions to problems
- minimises the risk of overlooking elements of the problem.[4]

The doctors' questionnaire

Use the following for ideas: insert your own headings that relate to your practice.

Photocopy these pages for the doctors and manager in the practice to complete a copy each, individually and anonymously. These can then be collected in for analysis.

 For the doctors and manager

The pressures

1 What are the pressures in your job?

Here are some statements that have been made at different times about GP practices. How far do you agree or disagree? Which one is most important to you? Weight each one in order of importance, with 10 being a big issue, 0 being insignificant.

- Lack of time.
- Personalities and management style/role.
- Financial issues.
- Partnership differences.
- Uncertainty around future direction of practice.
- Poor organisation.
- Pressures from external agencies, e.g. Health Authority, PCGs, the government.
- Staff shortages.
- Problems with premises.
- Other . . . .

Core value systems

2 Which of the following motivates you at work?

- Money.
- The social aspect of work.
- Responsibilities.
- Being given initiatives.
- Intellectual stimulation.
- The caring aspect of the job.
- Other ....

What would you say are the values that are important to you? (Some common examples include love, money, health, success, children, freedom.)

My core values are ....

The vision

3 What is your vision for your practice?

○ If the practice were a car (or a drink, or a piece of furniture) what would it be now?

○ What car/drink would you prefer it to be?

Values

4 What do you value most about the practice?

○   In your opinion, what are the three best things about this practice?

1

2

3

○   Name the three worst things about this practice.

1

2

3

5 What changes do you think would improve the way the surgery works?

Weight the following areas of change, with 0 being of no importance and 5 being most important.

- Premises.
- Good management.
- Finance.
- Better organisation.
- Communication.

6 What single thing would improve your working life?

7 What are your expectations of a manager? What would you like a practice manager to do?

1

2

3

4

5

Goal setting

8 What do you see are the obstacles to change?

Using pictures

It is a good idea to think creatively about the situation you are now in. In drawing, you use the right hand side of your brain (the left hemisphere is thought to be responsible for language and cognition, the right for visual imagery, intuition and older, instinctive memories from childhood). Tap into your intuition and draw how you see your life at present. Use numbers, colours, people, arrows, 'think bubbles' or shapes to sketch out what you see. Illustrate some of the geography, some of the activities, some elements of relationships, worries, conflicts, responsibilities, etc.

Here is one example.

In this picture the doctor is on a ship, steaming forward to a new life as a PCG chair. She has left behind her practice, partners and staff on a desert island, where only radio communication is possible. Her family of small children are on another island, and although there is easy boat access visiting times are limited. One of her partners is not on board the cruise ship, and constantly disrupts her progress by cutting across in a speedboat. Another partner is sunbathing on a nearby yacht, relaxing with a drink in hand.

Draw a picture illustrating how you see yourself at work and what you see as the influences and supports around you.

9 Who do you see in your immediate support network?

This picture shows models of people to illustrate support networks more clearly:

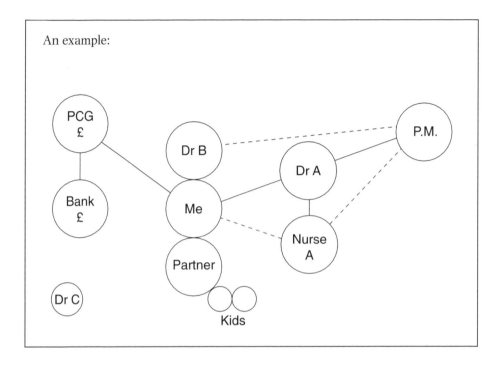

An example:

Your support network:

10 From your picture, write down some of the positive and negative influences you noted.

Positive	*Negative*

11 In this section, note some possible ways to solve the problems.

Write down any possible solution, however improbable or seemingly impossible. Do you see anything that could be done to make things better? Any idea, cost is no barrier (when brainstorming you do not impose limits – these come when you modify your choices later).

Solutions

Next steps

12 Now refer back to your own pictures and some of those solutions. Write down any solutions that, in retrospect, you feel would work.

1

2

3

4

5

Close your eyes and write the solution on an imaginary doorway in front of you. Stand in front of the door and walk through it. What do you find on the other side?

Having collected in your questionnaires, set up an evening or weekend meeting to elicit more information from the partners and the manager.

Additional questions for a partnership meeting

 **For the team**

Requirements for the meeting:
- facilitation skills or an independent facilitator
- all the key practice members, including the manager
- plenty of time (at least three hours)
- a flip chart
- pens
- patience
- courage
- honesty.

USE A FLIP CHART TO NOTE ALL THE RESPONSES

1 What do you see as the three main achievements of previous years?

2 What is your vision of the business?
- Staff.
- Clinical.
- Finance.
- Premises.

Notes

Be realistic, e.g. you may aim to provide an exceptional service to patients but your practice cannot support this.

Think of the practice situation. Are you in:

- an area of outstanding natural beauty
- an inner city
- the suburbs
- an area of rural deprivation?

Do you need or want to build expertise in:

- treating the elderly
- children and families
- those with mental health problems?

Do you want to provide:

- an exceptional/competitive service/GMS only
- any special services, like physiotherapy, counselling or family planning
- holistic healthcare?

3 What are your overall aims for yourself within the business?

- Do you want to rely totally on the income generated or do you have alternative income sources?
- Do you want to expand? When? Into what?
- How many days a week do you want to work and what is your ceiling on the number of patients you wish to see in a day?

4 What is your background?

What influences your thinking; have you developed any particular clinical expertise?

SWOT analysis

Here we take a look at the practice strengths and weaknesses, and ask what the team perceive the opportunities and threats to be. Which of these present obstacles to change?[5]

Notes

- Issues the practice has to deal with may either be under its control or not. They may be external to the practice (such a threat may be an adjoining GP practice) or within the practice itself (a strength may be the nursing team, for example).
- Controllable issues are internal, usually generated by the business owners and the business itself.
- Non-controllable issues include national or local issues out of the practice control.
- Most outside opportunities also carry a threat – even if just to stability – all change is difficult to manage.
- Some of the current forces driving change in the health service can represent a strength and a weakness. A recession, for example, may mean less public money and an increased use of the health services, but could also be an opportunity for practices wishing to increase their list size or practise private medicine.
- Everyone in the practice will have a different shape and size, and this cannot be changed but managed to bring out the strengths and minimise the weaknesses. For example, in a young practice youth brings freshness, enthusiasm, clinical commitment and expertise. However, family commitments take their toll on individuals' ability to keep fully aware of their responsibilities, particularly the management accountabilities of general practice.

Internal factors: controllable

Here we look at the partnership:

- strengths and weaknesses
- leadership skills
- influencing skills
- intellectual skills
- emotional commitment
- personality factors
- energy levels
- team skills
- ability to face change.

How far are the partners committed to having direct input into the running of the practice? What are the strengths in the practice? Who:

- manages their time well (but may be controlling or demanding)
- learns from mistakes, and has insight (but may be over sensitive)
- holds the vision for the practice
- leads and/or motivates
- is computer literate
- has financial acumen
- has networking skills
- has health service contacts
- freshness, enthusiasm and commitment
- has clinical expertise
- is fully aware of the responsibilities and accountabilities of general practice
- is committed to keeping within budget
- has direct input into the running of the practice
- is well liked by staff
- is demanding
- is creative and visionary (but may hold unrealistic expectations)
- tends to be dysfunctional in the practice (but may be very brilliant)
- (if there are pressures of time) tends to be rude or out of control?

External factors: non-controllable

Which of these makes an impact on the practice?

- National/regional/local policies and plans.
- Economic factors: recession, lack of growth monies in the NHS.
- NHS Information and Technology Strategy.
- Social/cultural.
- Private sector.
- Drug companies.

Some external opportunities presenting themselves to ambitious GPs are tempting: enthusiastic, experienced and committed GPs can become involved in local medical political or clinical groups – the Local Medical Committee (LMC), Primary Care Groups (PCGs), etc.

There are benefits and disadvantages to this.

- Is time away from the business properly resourced?
- What about the time, energy and commitment to management not medicine?
- Do you feel current uncertainties around national and local direction create and maintain a climate of indecision?

These unsettling factors need containing and managing so clinicians feel there is enough time and energy left to practise medicine, and staff do not feel endlessly overwhelmed by change.

- ○ Have consultation and referral rates risen in your practice in recent years? Have you measured this? Have DNA rates risen recently? Note this, and some of the reasons for this, which could be:
    - an increase in available appointments
    - a trainee registrar joining the practice whose referral rate was extraordinarily high
    - any GP clinical specialties which are high cost (psychiatry and mental health, for example)
    - patients targeting the practice for certain specialties, e.g. mental health, paediatrics.

For an example of a SWOT analysis report, *see* the website.

Staff questionnaire

Use a questionnaire to ask staff how they feel about working in the practice. Ask all staff, from the most part time cleaner to the most senior nurse. For an example questionnaire, *see* the website.

For some additional questions for the practice manager, *see* the website.

 **For the whole team**

Viewing your organisation as if you were a visitor from a foreign land

To gain a fresh perspective on your workplace, and broaden your awareness of the sorts of things that are important to an organisation, ask yourself the following questions.[6]

1 What struck you as different when you first joined this organisation?

2 Think about another organisation with which you are familiar. What do you feel is interesting or odd about the way things are done here that would not be found or accepted elsewhere?

3 Tell about a recent event that would sum up or illustrate this organisation to an outsider.

4 What messages do people communicate in your organisation? What are the behaviours that lead people to be considered heroes, villains, fools?

5 What would happen if you tried to implement a new idea? What would you need to enable it to happen? Who would block it, hinder it, support it?

6 What do others say about your organisation? What impression do they go away with?

Response to questionnaires

Having collated the responses, present a brief overview or snapshot picture of the practice back to everyone at a meeting. Use this opportunity to tease out some more about the strengths and weaknesses, and begin to consider how the practice can solve some of these problems: brainstorm some solutions and mark these up as aims and objectives to be included in the business plan.

- Make it short and concise.
- Keep it to two pages of A4 if possible.
- Use plain English.
- Translate if you have non-English speakers in the practice.

The following example could serve as a blueprint.

The staff survey

x number of staff were surveyed. A total of *x* responses was received.

1 The pressures

Here are some statements that have been made at different times about GP practices. The graph shows how far you agree or disagree. Each one is weighted in order of importance, with the higher numbers indicating big issues for the practice.

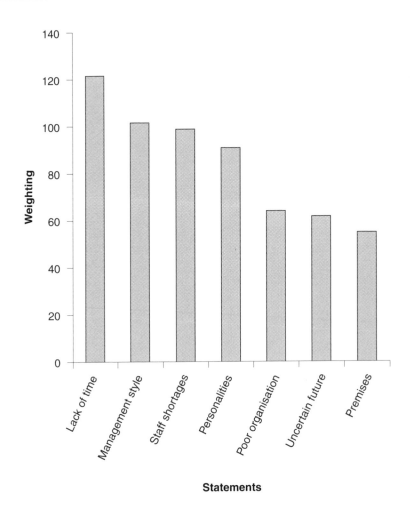

Figure 1.1 Work pressures.

Other issues mentioned:

- poor organisation
- difficulty obtaining information/decisions when needed
- lack of continuity between shifts
- heavy management style
- too much paperwork
- fatigue and pressure of work
- favouritism.

2 What motivates you at work?

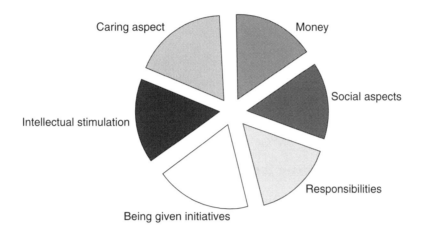

Figure 1.2 Practice motivations.

3 Do you feel cared for?

The Yes answers are shown as %.

- The practice is stretching and developing me.   82%
- The practice cares for its patients in the best possible way.   75%
- I feel safe in the workplace, not bullied or harassed, intimidated
  or discriminated against.   82%
- I feel happy and valued in my job.   73%

4 If the practice were a car (or a drink) what would it be?

- a bubble car – all vision, no power
- flat coke
- Volvo estate wagon
- Range Rover
- bucks without the fizz
- Ford escort
- an ancient BMW
- a re-sprayed boy racer
- banger
- flat Champagne.

5 What car/drink would you like it to be?

- top of the range people carrier, same driver
- Rolls-Royce
- Mercedes
- brand new Porsche convertible
- Champagne
- anything top of the range: smooth, expensive, efficient.

6 What single thing would improve your working life?

- extra staff
- a treatment room
- more filing space
- more time
- more filing clerks
- thanks for jobs well done
- better management
- more money
- no endless changes
- staff car park
- lunch breaks
- to be given more responsibility
- no disruptive doctors.

7 What would you like a practice manager to do?

- forward plan
- understand, maintain and support the practice
- staff/patient manager
- be the voice of the practice
- undertake training and appraisals
- facilitate consensus between the partners, enabling decisions and ensuring they are acted on
- be authoritative and calm in a crisis
- organisation
- be experienced, approachable, friendly
- to delegate
- no favouritism/treat all staff equally/be fair
- be full time if possible (consistency)
- oversee practice as a whole

- be flexible and open to new ideas
- day to day running of practice/hands on
- support the interests of all groups within practice
- communicate effectively with all staff.

8 Some of the good and bad things about the practice

Most frequently mentioned positives	*Most frequently mentioned negatives*
Friendly doctors	Favouritism
Caring	Conflicts
The premises	Time wasting/interruptions
Good communication	Constant changes
Enthusiasm and organisation	

More negatives:

- petty jealousies
- frustrations with partners
- not enough breaks
- poor decision making
- money issues
- moody staff
- no locum availability
- wait too long for appointments
- meetings held too frequently/infrequently
- no crêche facility
- not enough rooms
- relationship with PCT
- poor internal communication.

9 Some solutions

- expand/consolidate
- increase nursing time
- new partner
- more filing time
- additional secretarial support
- additional computer workstations
- in-house phlebotomy
- increase reimbursement levels

- stabilise the practice population
- reduce list size/freeze list.

Summary

The practice has come a long way in a very short time. There are many, many good things about *x* practice – the general consensus is that *x* (include all the positives, e.g. the premises are wonderful/the partners are caring and friendly/the staff are committed/it is well organised).

As with all practices, there are difficulties too (include the negatives, e.g. there is some favouritism/people complain of not being able to concentrate on their work/there are too many interruptions/communication could be better/decision making is poor/there is never enough time).

Staff would like their practice to provide a Rolls-Royce service, but this needs to be balanced realistically against resource constraints. Everyone wants to be able to work without constant change imposed on them, but this too is hard given the political nature of the NHS. However, while accepting personality differences are inevitable (everyone has their own 'shape' and way of doing things), difficult personality aspects can be managed, and the practice is united in its desire to begin to tackle some of the presenting problems.

Recommendations to the practice following the review

- The partnership needs to take a firmer role in decision making.
- Each partner needs to take on a named and joint responsibility (with the practice manager) for a key area of management, e.g. finance, premises, staff, clinical issues.
- Communication errors within the practice need to be minimised, everyone should know what is going on and who is responsible for what.
- The manager needs to be actively involved in clinical management, e.g. planning, monitoring and advising the partnership on clinical governance, systems management, alternative clinical management paths, and business development.
- The manager needs to be able to develop and deliver strategically, and manage the GPs, helping them clarify where they want to take their business, when and how.
- The practice needs to use its information system constructively and to allocate protected and paid time to effectively interrogate its database.

For other information to collect for your plan, *see* the website.

References

1   Department of Health (1998) *A First Class Service: quality in the new NHS*. DoH, London.

2   Pritchard P (ed.) (1981) *Patient Participation in General Practice*. RCGP Occasional Paper 17. RCGP, London.

3   Checkland P (1999) *Systems Thinking, Systems Practice*. Wiley, Chichester.

4   Bishop S and Taylor D (1994) *Developing Your Staff*. Pitman/Longman Training, London.

5   Ansoff H (1987) *Corporate Strategy*. Penguin, London.

6   Adapted from McLean A, Bath Associates.

CHAPTER 2

What is an organisation?

Having surveyed your practice, you will now have a very good idea about some of the big issues affecting it. Before we look at what is best to include in a business plan, it is worth revisiting the term *organisation*, as a business plan essentially is undertaken and written to check out, and reflect, the health of an organisation. In this chapter we begin to unpick some of the meanings behind this term.

In studying an organisation we need to look at, understand, predict and control human behaviour. Nothing happens in any organisation without people. But the study of organisations involves more than just the behaviour of people, this needs to be put in context. GPs are moving from a simple, single organisation to a far more complex one – one that needs to take on board many heavy external influencing forces to enable it to survive as a business. To fully understand your organisation, you need to have a broad understanding of:

- the process of management
- the organisational context and processes
- the interactions with the external environment, of which the organisation is part
- why people behave as they do.

The process of business planning will help take you through some of these issues. From your survey, you will now have a broad idea of some of the management processes in your organisation, and some idea of the motivations, aims and goals sought by those within it. Further work needs to be done to find out what impacts on your practice, and what influences behaviour within it. People do not work in isolation, their behaviour is influenced by the following.

⟹ **For the whole team**

The individual

○   Are the needs of individuals within your practice at odds with the demands made on them?

The group

Every member within your practice will be a member of one or more formal or informal groups.

○   Do you know which group you belong to?

The organisation

Structure is created by management to create order, to help establish relationships between people and to direct the efforts of the organisation towards the goals they have established. Behaviour is affected by these systems.

○   Who in the practice has the authority to create these structures?
○   Do they understand what they are doing and why?

The environment

○   What do you see as the biggest influence on general practice?

Organisations are, on the surface, influenced by many things:[1]

- service users
- technology
- formal goals
- facilities
- rules and regulations
- financial constraints
- surface competencies and skills
- scientific, social and cultural influences.

The behavioural aspects are more covert, and more troublesome:

- attitudes
- communication
- team processes
- personalities
- conflict
- political behaviour
- underlying competencies and skills.

It is the role of the manager to understand and integrate all these activities, to co-ordinate, encourage and improve systems and people, and ensure that people's work needs are satisfied. Does your manager have these skills?

What is culture?

Culture is another word which will keep cropping up as we analyse your organisation. Most people are unaware of just how much their culture affects them. General practice is influenced not just by the pervading external cultural factors[2] (language, values, religion, education, the law, economics, politics, technology, environment and attitudes), but by its own internal culture. The internal culture could be a medical one, heavily influenced by the history of the development of medicine. Here the values may be traditional (patriarchal and conservative), or the values may be set by others with different views and values: dominated by religion, family, feminism or ecology. In traditional organisations authority is legitimised by custom and a long standing belief in the natural right to rule. In charismatic organisations, authority is legitimised by a belief in the personal qualities of the leader, their strength and personality. In bureaucratic organisations, authority is based on an acceptance of the law and formal rules and impersonal principles.[3]

 For the whole team

How far do your personal values coincide with the practice values? How far do you seek to influence and change the practice values? Do you fit in, or are you lost? Are you aware of and do you understand your practice values with regard to the following:

- language
- education
- religion
- technology
- the law

- economics
- social organisation?

For the majority of staff in general practice, work is becoming less of a life-long function; contracts are more short term and flexible working patterns more common, people are less likely to feel a need to conform to traditional values. Most people work to pay the mortgage; the social function of work is becoming less important.

For GPs the picture is slightly more complex: prior to the NHS Act 1999 it was imperative that GPs in partnership understood and fitted in with the prevailing culture at work – most practice disputes and difficulties arise when people are seen not to 'fit in'. However, this may change as more GPs take up a salaried option, a choice which brings the individual more freedom to move on. If practices choose to take up PMS contracts, it will be more important than ever before for them to be seen to evaluate their cultural stance, and work together to achieve common core values.

Culture and leadership

Charles Handy, management guru, describes the 'ecology' of an organisation thus:

> 'The management of groups and individuals and the control of conflict, are all ways of managing the environment in order to influence behaviour and effect change.'[4]

Leadership styles can give us a clue to the type of culture within your organisation. Managers all have their own individual way of leading. In general practice, the culture is usually hierarchical, with the staff responsible to the manager, but accountable to the partners who own the business. Unless the manager is a partner too, the buck stops ultimately with the partners. If the management and partnership styles differ, difficulties can arise. The power base shifts, staff bypass the manager to clarify issues and management credibility and authority is lost. This weakens the organisation and can set up uncertainties and confusions as management is undermined.

There are several ways to manage. Most managers adopt a style that they feel comfortable with and that matches the expectations of the people they work for. Most move through the matrix of styles depending on the situation facing them. They move fluidly, almost unconsciously; sometimes they find themselves behaving in an autocratic way when their style is usually democratic; more often they adopt styles consciously depending on the situation facing them. For example, there is a need to be autocratic at times of rapid and imposed change or crisis – someone has to make decisions fast. Managers can afford to adopt a more diplomatic stance when time is on their hands and there is time to consult and debate. Each style carries its own strengths and weaknesses, and the reader will recognise their own approach.

 **For the whole team**

Can you recognise the style in your practice?

Autocratic

- This is safe and paternalistic.
- It carries a clear chain of command and authority.
- The divisions of work and hierarchy are fully understood by all.
- It works well in a crisis or in a situation where quick results are needed.
- The people who respond best to this style are those who need clear, detailed and achievable directives.

The autocratic manager must really be an expert in her field, as she receives little or no information from others – this can be dangerous in today's work environment of technological and organisational complexity.

The weaknesses are in the apparent efficiency of one way communication. Without feedback there is often misunderstanding, communication breakdown and costly errors. The critical weakness, however, is its effect on people – long gone are the days where the boss gave orders and people obeyed without question. Most people resent authoritarian rule and respond with resentment, resistance or sabotage. The authoritarian ruler does not really respect people and this causes low morale.

Bureaucratic

- There is a consistency of policy and operations.
- There is a sense of fairness and impartiality.
- People know and understand the rules.
- People feel secure.

Although directives, policies and rules are essential in any business – especially medicine where medico-legal parameters must be defined – there must be some flexibility, otherwise people react as they would to autocratic management. It is important to be flexible in situations where there should be exceptions to rules, to remember that policies represent legislation for the majority. Paralysis can result if the rules are ambiguous.

In public sector organisations generally there is a demand for treatment to be uniform, procedures to be regular, and there must be accountability for operations. This has led to adherence to specified rules and procedures which are now thought to be limiting, stifling flexibility, creativity and freedom. Of course, tried and tested rules and procedures help to ensure essential values and ethics, and help to ensure consistency and fairness.

Does your practice work in either of these ways? What do you see as the advantages and disadvantages of these approaches?

- Clear cut hierarchies and procedures.
- High levels of specialisation can be achieved.
- Uniformity of decisions and actions.
- A clear structure of authority.
- Good co-ordination.
- Rational, impersonal judgements.
- Life-long career expectations.
- Dependence on rules and regulations.

Or is your practice style:

Diplomatic

- Commonly seen in general practice.
- Manager has no real line of authority.
- Manager dependent on the skills of persuasion in getting the co-operation she needs.
- Manager takes time to explain rather than order. This has advantages in that people work more enthusiastically if given reasons for a task; they feel respected. The manager is rewarded by co-operation.

Often staff recognise the attempts to persuade rather than order as a sign of weakness and can lose respect for the manager. If the diplomacy fails and the manager fails to 'sell' the deal, this comes through to people as frank manipulation and hypocrisy, and is thus deeply resented and resisted. The manager has lost out by not having a clear cut line of authority – any attempt to then revert to a frank autocratic order has an obvious and disastrous effect on people.

Participative

- People participate in and help formulate a decision.
- People support decisions instead of fighting them.
- They work hard to make it work, because it becomes their idea.
- Group discussion is the norm.

This is currently thought to be by far the best way of leading, as staff have a key input into decision making so the manager benefits from a rich array of good information and ideas. Group discussion always improves decision making, and may actually help avert disaster. People are encouraged to develop, and contribute more to the organisation as a result – they also develop a sense of personal achievement and value. People work better and more enthusiastically when given a high level of freedom in contribution. The participative manager establishes a work climate which unleashes power and gives people recognition and a deep sense of personal value and self-esteem.

The down side is that the participative style takes an enormous amount of time, which is not often available to general practice. It can be inefficient if used inappropriately – if people are not able or committed enough to take on board the responsibility it releases. There are times when managers use this style as a way of devolving or abdicating responsibility. If not handled well, it can result in a complete loss of managerial control. Needless to say, if a manager needs to reject a recommendation, they should quickly explain why this had to happen, otherwise resentment occurs.

Free-rein

• Delegation optimises full use of time and resources.
• Many people are motivated to full effort when given freedom.

This carries a high degree of risk with very little managerial control. The manager needs to know the competence and integrity of her people and their ability to handle this kind of freedom. It is a level of management usually given only to senior managers in an organisation.

 **For the whole team**

What style would you prefer in your practice?[5]

○ I value stability in my job.
○ I like my life to be unpredictable.
○ I like to know exactly what is expected of me.
○ If I could afford it, I would prefer to be self employed or freelance.
○ Seniority is more important than performance in determining pay.
○ I prefer working for a big organisation.
○ Rules and procedures tend to frustrate me.
○ I like working flexibly.
○ I like uniforms.
○ Parking spaces should be allotted according to seniority.
○ Rules are meant to be broken.

Leadership versus management, or the manager as an enabler

There is a need in all organisations for 'individual linking pins who will bind groups together'.[4] The leader is not necessarily the manager. In fact in general practice, it is for the partners to lead and for the manager to *enable* this to happen by co-ordinating the change required. The leader visions, the manager controls.

In many practices, there is a tendency to lead with a predominantly autocratic, task-orientated style, but there is a shift where some of the younger partners are looking to share the control, moving the organisation toward a more modern, participative and supportive management style. Where a more direct style of management is preferred, there can be problems.

Supportive style leadership

- Related to lower turnover and grievance rates.
- Related to subordinate satisfaction.
- Results in less inter-group conflict.
- Is often the style preferred (and expected) by subordinates in today's work culture.

Directive leadership

- Directive leadership could increase productivity, but only if the task is routine and repetitive.
- Some people prefer a highly structured style, to be led.
- Could be the most productive style when managing a crisis.

Organisational structure

Small businesses, such as general practice, do not really benefit from a structural analysis, i.e. whether the organisational hierarchy is flat or tall, whether the work is divided by function or location, etc. We need not concern ourselves with structural theory, but it is interesting to consider some of the consequences of bad structure. First of all, acquaint yourself with what is considered to be the structure in your workplace.

> ⇨ **For the whole team**

Draw a picture showing your organisational structure. The ideal may look something like this:

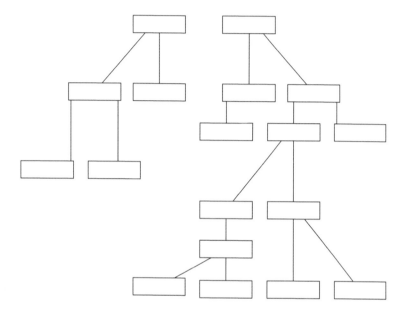

Figure 2.1 Organisational structure.

Write in where your manager belongs, and the partners, nursing staff, medical secretaries, reception staff, cleaner and so on.

Then, using the picture analogy on p. 14, draw the reality in the box on p. 44.

What are the consequences of badly designed structure?

Child[6] points out there are a number of problems that mark the struggling organisation, all of which mark rising costs as well as an unhappy workforce.

For the whole team

Mark off the following problems identified in your workplace:

- ○ inconsistent and arbitrary decisions
- ○ poor delegation
- ○ no job descriptions
- ○ no appraisal system or formal assessment of performance
- ○ competing and conflicting pressures
- ○ poor support systems for managers and supervisors
- ○ change unsupported
- ○ management not visible and accessible
- ○ a general fear of failure in the organisation
- ○ management information, especially financial, poorly communicated
- ○ people don't feel free to talk.

Low morale
- ○ poor communication
- ○ lack of relevant, timely information to the right people
- ○ overloading of decision makers
- ○ failure to re-evaluate past decisions
- ○ poor delegation.

Poor decision making
- ○ conflicting goals
- ○ cross purposes
- ○ lack of clarity on objectives and priorities
- ○ lack of liaison
- ○ no team working
- ○ breakdown between planning and the actual work.

Conflict and lack of co-ordination
- ○ failure to forecast external change
- ○ failure to give adequate attention to strategy and innovation
- ○ failure to give attention to the importance of planning for and managing change
- ○ inability to identify market change and research into possible technological solutions.

Poor response to new opportunities

Influences on the development of culture

⟹ **For the manager**

Think about these key influences on the culture of general practice[7]

○ History – when and why did the NHS form? What was the background to general practice development? How are GPs seen in relation to their consultant colleagues?

○ What do you see as the primary function of general practice? What is the importance of reputation or the range of services provided?

○ What are prime goals and objectives – money, patient care or excellence?

○ Size and location – what are the communication difficulties presenting? What about opportunities for development?

○ Management influences – are you responsive to change? Is anyone else in the practice?

○ What are the routines, rituals and stories told within the organisation and within the NHS as a whole?

○ What symbols are used by the practice – any logos, titles, language that represent the practice to outsiders?

The organisational context

Organisations come in all shapes and sizes. Consider the differences between a bank, a hospital and a leisure centre; or a general practice and airport. There are common factors. There are always two broad categories of resources:

- **non-human** – physical assets, materials, equipment, facilities
- **human** – people's abilities and skills, and their influence.

In all organisations, whatever their size, we see the efforts and interactions of people working to achieve objectives through a structure which is directed and controlled by management.

Formally, organisations operate with organisational charts, policies and procedures. Informally they operate through personal friendships, grapevines, emotions, power games, informal relationships and leadership.

The basic components of an organisation that we need to be aware of are:

- operating component – comprising the people who actually do the work or provide the service – the clinical and reception team, for example
- administrative component – comprising managers and supervisors.

Traditionally, organisations can be distinguished in terms of two generic groups:

- private enterprise
- public sector.

General practice still, currently, and sometimes uncomfortably, straddles the two. While the Red Book contract still stands, there will always be an inherent tension between the care-taking quality and the need to make money.

This government recognises that GP contracts are outdated and limiting. There will be a big extension of quality based contracts for GPs in general, and single-handed GPs in particular. The way family doctors have been rewarded has remained largely unchanged since 1948. The fees and allowances relate to the number of patients registered and (the government considers) insufficiently to the services provided and the quality of those services. By April 2002 it is expected nearly a third of GPs will be working to a Personal Medical Contract, where quality standards are in-built. By 2004 both local Personal Medical Services and national arrangements are set to operate within a single contractual framework, completely amending the current Red Book contract. Salaried GPs will become more common, and with this there will be a built-in expectation for GPs to accept and adhere to certain common quality standards.

> $\Longrightarrow$ **For the whole team**

Think about the key characteristics within your organisation[7]

- Size – small or very large?
- Formality – informal or highly structured?
- Activities – what tasks are performed and by whom?
- Complexity – simple or complicated?
- People skills – types of people involved: class, education, age, etc.
- Location – single or multiple?
- Goals – what is the organisation trying to accomplish?

Stakeholder analysis

Strategy in general practice is still partially governed by profit, but an important and growing influence is the government. Strategy in the public sector is governed by broader public policy issues such as politics, monopoly supply, bureaucracy and finite resources. The power and influence exercised should also be tempered by responsible and ethical management; the organ-isation, by default, accepts and assumes responsibility for public good.

Here we take a look at some of the influencers in general practice, the 'stakeholders'. These are people who have an interest and/or are affected by the goals or activities of the organisation. Who are your stakeholders and how do they exert their power and influence?

 For the whole team

Who are your stakeholders and what are their concerns?

○ Employees – what are your joint needs?
○ The providers of finance – public and private (expect a fair service for bearing the risk of investment).
○ Consumers – customers and patients (who want value for money, good care, efficiency, full service access).
○ Community and environment (concerned with the siting of buildings, pollution, transport, waste or research).
○ Government – both assists and limits in what ways?

There are ethical concerns that stakeholders should be interested in. Who of the above will stake an interest in these?

○ Workers' rights.
○ Patient safety.
○ Accounting practices.
○ Whistle-blowing by staff.
○ Research.
○ Doctors' remuneration.
○ Discrimination.
○ Privacy and security of data.
○ Trade union relationships.

Look on the website to see some of the influences that are pushing primary care into new ways of working. These new ways are not always welcomed or even seen to be possible, by those expected to work with and manage the change.

Forcefield analysis

If you list opposing groups of stakeholders and draw arrows between them, you will see illustrated some of the influences or people driving the cultural change on the one hand, with those resisting the change on the other. One of the management roles is to successfully manage the change, to ensure we move beyond the status quo by either reducing the impact of some of the driving forces (enabling the resisters to move forwards), or influencing those resisting so that they come to realise the need for change themselves. One of the biggest learning points in doing this exercise is to see how far we push change, without enabling people to take it on board themselves.

 For the whole team

Who drives the change in your organisation?

External

- political (national/regional)
- local authority
- economic
- IT
- social and cultural
- private healthcare
- drug companies.

Internal

Who has the biggest influence/powerful leadership?
- practice team
- practice culture.

What are the threats?
- threat to income
- threat to stability
- threat of upheaval
- fear of the unknown
- fear of losing control/autonomy.

 Some of the barriers to overcome:

- emotional commitment
- intellectual commitment
- skill required for change.

So why do we need to study culture, and forcefield analysis, and stakeholder analysis and...?

If your practice has a person-centred culture, with a powerful and autocratic style of leadership and management attempting to manage, change will not be successful. There will be an equally powerful force within the practice resisting this type of management, wanting to be managed, but not as yet knowing by whom or how. There will be others within the practice who make formal or informal bids for leadership at different times, which complicates matters even further!

Your practice may work as a 'galaxy of stars', with each GP making a bid for leadership at different times. It is never clear either, within this type of practice, who leads and chaotic management results. There will also always be powerful internal and external forces pushing all practices into change, which is viewed by some in the organisation as positive, and by others as negative. Recognise yourself?

There are clear implications for action, as these practices are in a state of chaos; but action can only succeed personal learning. The costs to such practices (of resisting change) would be dear; the benefits to the organisation huge and fundamental, both financial (the practice could grow into the role expected of it) and personal (less stress and conflict for those working within the organisation).

However, change is painful and difficult, and needs to be managed well for everyone to be comfortable with the process. It is particularly difficult for those within the practice who have the formal authority to lead and manage conferred on them, as their preferred style of management is task not people-centred. It will be especially hard for them to let go of their present authority and need to control. For these people, we need to be especially aware of the need to offer support through change and the attendant mourning process.

It is clear that many practices are now too big to be managed successfully and sensitively by traditional means. The sort of business analysis recommended in this book may lead to an awareness of cultural problems. There are too many time pressures that lead both the managers and partners to manage badly, in an autocratic, chaotic or uninformed way, even if their preferred style might be more enabling. There is often too little understanding of management and organisation to enable managers to manage successfully.

Each practice has to review how their organisation works, and their management role. This means involving the whole team, looking at those tasks that can be taken on by other leaders in the organisation (the office manager, the accountant or the partners). Whatever decisions are made, it is imperative that the whole organisation is involved at whatever level, and for everyone to be clear about those decisions.

There is not necessarily ever a best or right way to do things – this depends on the task and the state of the organisation at the time. Whatever option is chosen there needs to be awareness and flexibility around managing both the process and outcome.

References

1   Hellriegel D, Slocum J and Woodman R (2000) *Organizational Behaviour* (9e). South Western College Publishing, Minneapolis-St Paul.

2   Welford R and Prescott K (1994) *European Business: an issue-based approach* (2e). Pitman, London.

3   Weber M (1964) *The Theory of Social and Economic Organisation.* Collier Macmillan, London.

4   Handy C (1993) *Understanding Organisations.* Penguin, London.

5   DuBrin A (1978) *Human Relations: a job-oriented approach.* Prentice-Hall, London.

6   Child J (1988) *Organisation: a guide to problems and practice* (2e). Chapman, London.

7   Mullins LJ (1999) *Management and Organisational Behaviour* (5e). Financial Times/Pitman, London.

Further reading

Blades M (1992) Modelling in strategic analysis. *Health Service Management.* **August**.

Mullins LJ (1999) Management and Organisational Behaviour (5e). Financial Times/Pitman, London.

Pattison S (1991) Masters of change. *Health Service Journal.* **October**.

CHAPTER 3

What to include in a business plan

We have now considered some of the invisible factors that impact on a workplace. We have a broad understanding of the nature of organisations and culture. We know why it is important to consider these influences. You will also now have a clearer idea about your own practice's aims and objectives and the goals and motivations of the people within the organisation. You will certainly have a clearer idea about some of the problems!

Now it is time to flesh out some of the detail and clarify how you as a practice are going to tackle those problems. In this chapter we begin with an overview of the practice aims and objectives: those aims and objectives that you have identified through your practice survey. Again, it is important to write these down, so this chapter looks at what to include in a business plan and gives you some ideas for presentation.

A good plan should be:

- focused
- clear
- simple
- measurable
- time bound
- agreed by everyone.

The first section of your business plan would include the mission statement (the aims and objectives that you have identified for the practice), and an executive summary.

The header page should include the title, year of production and some basic details about the practice (name, address and partners). Look on the website for an example of this and the contents page.

The summary

The practice mission statement

This statement encapsulates the vision of the business, its aims and objectives. It can be used to give a flavour of the organisation, the values and commitments that will be reflected in the patient literature. Remember to include something about the practice commitment to staff; the NHS Plan will be looking closely at the way NHS employers treat their staff. Practices will be signing up to a new Performance Framework for Human Resources, and assessed against performance targets (*Improving Working Lives*).

 For the whole team

Reflect for a minute on your collective goals

○   To enhance patient partnerships?
○   To be the leading practice in the area?
○   To grow with the 'industry'?
○   To be the most efficient?
○   To sustain profitability?
○   To work well and play hard?

Here is the opportunity to expand a little on the service you offer, your aims for that service:

> *We aim to provide an exceptional and competitive/family orientated/holistic service.*

Your overall aim for the business:

> *To be comfortably reliant on the income generated from our work within x years/to enable all the partners to retire at 50/to expand the business to the point where we are working in partnership with other lead members of the PHCT or complementary practitioners, etc.*

Your overall aims for staff:

> *We believe that staff are our greatest resource, and we seek to prove that the practice is investing in training and development. We believe we work in a climate that reduces absences and accidents, and tackles discrimination and harassment at source.*

Describe the service you aim to offer, to whom, and any special services offered, like physiotherapy, counselling or family planning. The aims are usually both financial and clinical – you may want to improve clinical practice, sharpen the practice management styles, or develop your clinical expertise. Identify here if the practice priority is to sign up to a PMS contract, or have a mix of salaried and self-employed practitioners. Your immediate concerns may be to generate and maintain a good profit margin. For an example, *see* the website.

⇒ **For the doctors**

Are your business aims family, financial or clinically focused?

Briefly write your own vision here:

Practice aims and objectives

Describe the service in more detail, any products you will use, sell or provide (special equipment, an in-house pharmacy or a travel clinic). Include where you work from, what kind of service you aim to offer, etc.

What are your overall aims for the practice? Do you want to rely totally on a Red Book income, or to have alternative income sources? Do you want to expand and work under a PMS contract? When? If single-handed, do you ever plan to work in partnership with others? How many days a week do you want to work ideally? What is your ceiling on the number of patients you wish to see in a day? Do you want your business to totally support or supplement your present lifestyle?

Practices commonly are uncertain whether to sit tight or develop further. General practice is often the victim of its own success, and many practices now need to look at ways of rationing non-essential or non-profit making services while maintaining their best practice objectives. Within practices there is often tension between the need to maintain list sizes through new registrations and the more generic work. A glut of new registrations present significant problems to practices. Clinically, the workload increases as many new problems are identified during the health checks, most of which do not attract target payments but nonetheless increase the workload – referrals, investigations, chronic disease programmes, etc.

 Practices need to be clear about their list size targets and manage within their decision.

Begin to unpick the detail of the business. Look on the website for details of a hypothetical partnership of young GPs whose main medical focus is holistic.

Note here the five main aims for your business as identified in your practice survey:

1

2

3

4

5

Common problems

Can you see your practice here?

Key considerations for most practices are:

- poor communication
- whether to consolidate or expand
- the need to skill-up management
- how to use information systems constructively
- the need to delegate clinically and managerially
- GPs need to measure their role in taking responsibility for their business
- the need to improve resource management and develop appropriate management systems.

Problem number one: communication breakdowns

Visions are impractical if unshared or not agreed by all parties. New ideas are more likely to succeed if shared, owned and understood by everybody. So often in general practice, ideas and plans are thought up in isolation, rarely by the whole practice. More often than not the idea takes hold and suddenly, with no discussion, the staff are informed there is to be an extra clinic, or the lunchtime session moved to early afternoon, or a new telephone system is to be bought.

 Change is difficult to manage at the best of times, but unless everyone is part of this type of discussion, sabotage is common and the plan will fail.

If someone in the practice tries out the new idea, and it succeeds, and especially if it costs, the PCT/PCG is approached for money. Rarely are the ideas talked through with interested stakeholders first.

 Sharing the plan first with external lead professionals helps clarify some of the wider issues, and firms up the proposals so that everyone involved can see whether any new plans are going to be viable or not.

Most GPs work reactively, so much of what goes on in general practice happens almost by chance, and big changes are rarely planned.

 Practices need to consider what their priorities are, and what they can afford over the next 2–5 years, then stage the development, marking each target with an aim (what the plan is) and objective (how to map the outcome).

Partnership responsibilities

Most doctors enter general practice because they are individualists; team players tend to gravitate towards hospital work. Doctors within general practice either enjoy taking the responsibility for establishing and promoting a successful business, or they (mistakenly) see general practice as a softer option, and prefer to work more gently, perhaps part time. Partly because of this, it is common to find partnerships struggling with decision making. Throughout the land there are practice managers tearing their hair out as, having distributed the partnership meeting minutes, one by one the partners, having agreed to do one thing, do something else.

Difficult personality traits lead to another problem: individual doctors taking either a too active or lesser role in taking responsibility for managing key problems and developing ownership of their business. Rarely is a balance struck. Partners often find it difficult to take on ownership of their business; they let it drift with no-one in charge. Or they take complete charge, and never delegate.

Lack of vision

Most practices aim to provide a fast, flexible and friendly service to their patients. They aim for an evidence-based and accountable approach to the delivery of care. Most try to ensure practice resources are targeted appropriately. GPs generally aim to be professional, respectful, honest, considerate and courteous. However, some practices hope to do all this without any management involvement at all! The GPs think if they are friendly and committed, this is enough. They work hard but forget that the above can only happen with good organisation and planning ahead.

Operationally, almost all practice systems are now risk assessed and practices are managing risk well. However, in order to minimise risk most practices need to address the major strategic issues and not simply concentrate on the operational management issues.

 Practices need to define the long and short term aims for their business.

Not all visions will be compatible. There needs to be agreement within the partnership to define mutually acceptable aims.

For an example description of a strategic vision, *see* the website.

Executive summary

This summarises the whole document, and will be written last. It identifies those issues you need to consider having evaluated your business. It takes an honest look at the practice strengths and weaknesses, and will, in recognition of the NHS Plan, represent the collective view of the whole practice team. The key recommendations appear at the end of this summary.

Executive summary

Here you summarise the **main aims and objectives** for your practice for the year ahead. Discuss the areas you have identified from the initial practice survey that you wish to develop or maintain, and the areas you want to see improvement in.

These may be in operational systems, for example you may wish to improve the way you plan and monitor practice finances or you may wish to improve the day to day running of the practice. However you must be specific, e.g. '*We aim to reduce internal staff costs through undergoing a skill mix review, and develop robust, less bureaucratic ways of managing the practice.*'

You may wish to develop strategically, by increasing your involvement with the local PCGs or PCTs, for example, or by signing up to a PMS contract.

Outline how you hope to **achieve these aims**; the objectives will be detailed within the bulk of the plan. Describe how the practice will be addressing major issues during the year: for example, how to manage the enormous increase in consultation rates; whether or not to reduce the list size. How are you going to improve public accountability? Will you be looking at rationing services? What is high on the practice agenda?

Note some of the practice's weaknesses and summarise how you plan to tackle them over the year to come, for example: '*The practice historically over-uses imaging and pathology services.*'

How do you plan to solve this? How will you achieve your aims: '*We will agree access protocols with our main provider that limit routine referrals by 10% in the following specialties: pathology and imaging. The practice manager will take a much more active involvement in monitoring and advising the partners on alternative clinical management paths.*'

Note any other management plans: '*The practice's performance will be scrutinised with the partners monthly at a performance review meeting.*'

Use this space to recall some of your business aims:

For a further example of an executive summary, *see* the website.

We now move on to the next stage of the business plan.

The service, premises and equipment

 For the doctors and manager

Here you expand further on:
- the partnership background
- what influences their thinking
- the expectations of the service offered
- any clinical expertise they have developed
- what market they hope to capture
- the practice boundary
- the qualifications of all key clinical and managerial staff
- what background work supports the business.

Staff

You may wish to summarise who your staff are, and their roles and responsibilities. Include the staff or organisational chart as an appendix, and do not forget to include the attached staff, community nurses and so on. It would be good to include a chart demonstrating key staff skills and any training needs.

Write down anything that each member of staff has done previously that may support you in your work. One may have an additional business qualification, or be a trained acupuncturist...

What do you know about your team? Were you surprised? Should you be?

Where is your market? Are there other practices similarly placed and equipped? How will you offer something unique?

Premises

Over 3000 GP premises are to be refurbished or replaced, and over 2000 new GPs will be working by 2004. Five hundred one-stop primary care centres are to be developed. There are plans to phase out single-handed practices.

Where do you work and what are your plans for future development? Could your premises support co-professionals: a consultant, social care staff, a dentist or optician or one of the new graduate mental health professionals? Could you house a rapid response community team?

Describe your premises – sell them:

Example

'The practice aims to provide a service to patients from Bristol South and surrounding areas. The practice is sited in an area of outstanding natural beauty/inner city/rural deprivation and is thus developing some expertise in treating the elderly/children and families and those with mental health problems.'

'The practice provides a service to just under 6000 patients from Rye and Winchelsea. It is an early Victorian brick and flint building adjacent to a small independent school situated in the heart of the ancient town of Rye, close to (and within walking distance of) local amenities (post office, pub, church, station and police station). The building is leased and has been attractively restored to modern standards, whilst retaining some of its early character. It is spacious and friendly and has excellent accessibility.'

Premises and finance

Premises

○   Are they part rented or leased?
○   Are they privately owned?
○   Are there any ownership issues?
○   Are you happy with the lease arrangements or rental agreement?

Finance

○   Is the practice part of the cost rent scheme?
○   Is private initiative finance expected?
○   Are you aware of the NHS Local Improvement Finance Trust (LIFT)? Could you benefit?
○   What are the future needs and developments planned for the building?
○   Are you in an area of deprivation?
○   Will your practice gain from new, and fairer, resource allocations?
○   Could your practice gain from one of the 200 Personal Medical Service schemes being allocated?

 Ownership problems are common. Put this on your list of priorities to sort.

The service

The partnership as a resource

Within the NHS Plan is a modernisation agency to be set up to address the needs of patients, and help local clinicians and managers meet that need. This agency will encourage streamlining services and sharing skills, develop best practice and make sure national protocols and care pathway plans are followed. Practices need to note where they are now, and whether they have the resources to meet the new needs. If you are considering developing services, think of the resource implications.

•   What about the primary care expectation for nurses to see patients within 24 hours, and GPs to see patients within 48 hours? When can you achieve this and how?
•   A cardiovascular specialist GP will need access to echocardiography and exercise testing facilities. A locum or additional partner will have to cover for them. What about the increased prescribing costs?
•   Have you got the capacity for the new retirement MOTs? What about the increased prescribing costs?

- Practices will need to complete an accreditation process before they can apply for any new contracts. Once done, they will be able to bid to provide a service to patients from other practices.

⟹ **This whole section is for the doctors and manager**

Consider the following issues. These are both for yourself, and for your report:

- how many partners
- how many sessions worked
- use of locums
- appointment availability and DNA rates
- use and description of deputising service
- any outside paid or committee work, and non-NHS work or private work
- specialist qualifications, clinical duties and skills
- training practice.

For an example, *see* the website.

Continue with:

- partnership history
- description of partnership agreement
- general description of income generation
- income generation (through GMS work only?)
- surgery based private work (medical insurances, cremation certificates, passports, etc.)
- outside work – are the monies pooled and shared?

Example

The partnership is emerging from a difficult history and is now building afresh with new premises. I recommend the partners draw up a partnership agreement with the aid of their solicitor, using GMC guidelines. This will act as a contract of employment for each partner and clarify partnership maternity rights, holiday cover arrangements, sick leave agreements, etc.

The partnership rely totally on the income generated through GMS work and surgery based private work (medical insurances, cremation certificates, passports, etc.). Outside work is not pooled, shared, or invested in the practice. I recommend this is reconsidered in the light of the wish to expand the practice services.

 Think more about how you are going to meet the new recommendations for funding GMS work. Start meeting and planning ahead for the changes now.

 Has your practice got a partnership agreement? Why not?

If outside work happens, and the work is done during practice time, then the money is usually pooled as the other partners will be providing cover in the practice for the absent doctor. Having an outside interest helps to add variety to the routine of daily work as well as bringing in additional income.

Continue with:

- aims to expand service
- aims to change GP contract: PMS contracts, salaried GPs, etc.
- ambitions and limitations
- development of clinical academic/research base
- developing or setting up specialist clinics for other practices to refer into
- alternative community prescribing project
- if single-handed, possibility of joining up with other single-handers to share resources.

For examples demonstrating partnership aims and ambitions, *see* the website.

Has the practice already identified any possible restrictions to taking up an offer of a PMS contract?

1

2

3

4

Clinical

Describe the practice clinical service in more detail. Use referral analysis to support your claims. By April 2001 every practice and PCG/T was required to have in place systems to monitor referral rates.

- Discuss the practice population.
- What are the identifiable clinical problems?
- Problem patients and problems with referring to secondary care.
- Secondary care waiting lists.

For an example of clinical pressures, *see* the website.

 Most practices do not use their nurses enough. Plan what you can delegate to them, set up supporting protocols for triage, prescribing and patient management programmes.

Support this with additional documents, included here or in the appendices:

- practice referral rates
- referral analysis
- age/sex register
- DNA analysis
- appointment availability.

Identify any other service developments or changes.

Use of NHS Direct

Note your use of NHS Direct or deputising services. For further information contact NHS Direct at: www.nhsdirect.nhs.uk

Patient consultation rates and access arrangements

Detail how you make your surgery accessible, and if you have improved access. Link the process to CHI expectations, quality team development (*see* below) and revalidation. It is expected that each practice will have an action plan, linked to the local Health Action Plan, that outlines how they are to improve accessibility.

Quality Team Development is a technique devised by the RCGP. It looks at:

- the work of entire PHCTs
- ease of getting appointments
- quality of premises
- confidentiality within the practice
- use of patient surveys.

Use of health promotion contracts might include:

- accident prevention
- sexual health
- carer support
- mental health
- green issues (transport, clean air and recycling policies).

Note if and how you have improved access (offer same day appointments) by:

- open, unbooked appointments
- having one doctor each morning devoted to seeing emergencies only
- having nurse triage appointments.

Identify if you have any special client groups to cater for, and if you have made special plans to include them in your improved access arrangements. For example:

We have improved access to our services for our learning disabled patients by:

- *reviewing screening requirements and including annual screening for mental/ visual/thyroid problems*
- *updating and improving our protocol for determining consent for treatment*
- *listing local support groups and specialist services available.*

There is a challenge here: PCG/Ts will both support and scrutinise practice performances.

PCG/Ts:

- prefer to apply local procedures
- rely on co-operation from GPs
- need to put patients first
- support the new culture to address performance
- define clear mechanisms for sharing sensitive information with other organisations
- look for clinicians and managers to work together.

Make a note of any mechanisms your practice has employed to reduce or manage increased service demands. Note the percentage of:

- repeat scripts
- telephone consultations
- inappropriate follow-ups
- any work with other agencies, e.g. youth services for sexual health service
- open surgeries
- practice nurse/community nurse skill mix
- dentistry, optometry and pharmacy within the practice
- use of NHS Direct
- use of walk-in centres (64% of patients who use these are non-registered patients living in a different area, and only 2% need a GP).

If you are a group practice, describe the way you work. There is no reason why individual partners cannot keep their own list to maintain a preferred model of single-handed practice.

Note your use of locums, and note particularly if any non-principal working within the practice is asked to adhere to practice protocols. It would be good practice to ask your locum workers to:

- be proactive
- improve their competencies
- analyse complaints and compliments

- analyse any changes in patient care
- analyse unexpected outcomes
- request feedback from referrals or investigations
- ask partners for feedback on interesting or significant outcomes.

Primary care is developing. General practice no longer simply manages acute disease but is also expected to:

- manage access
- prescribe
- manage chronic disease
- liaise and integrate with social care
- develop intermediate care
- develop early discharge referrals
- manage population based public health improvements
- be a resource manager – it holds the public purse.

Good GPs are therefore expected to:

- be available
- be accessible
- have technical skills
- have excellent communication skills and interpersonal attributes
- provide co-ordinated care
- provide continuity of care
- provide personal care
- identify patients at risk through audit and monitoring
- gather evidence
- use this evidence/data to decide what needs action
- act and review their action.

Mark off where this happens, and identify your limitations in achieving this. You are probably short on staff: prove it. You are probably short of funds: specify why you need these and for what. You do have the ability and resources to change. You are able to organise yourself both within the practice and locally, and you can harness local knowledge. Make this your aim.

Health needs report

(*See* also Chapters 9 and 10.) This process will help you identify the practice approach and understanding of clinical governance and NSFs. An annual report can be appended to the business plan, or can be written to stand alone. This is a report that gives an overview of individual practice needs and summarises recommendations for action. The report would include the following.

Practice overview

Link with your business plan to define your mission statement and note the principles that guide your practice.

o   Do you have a holistic approach to health, where health is defined as a sense of physical, mental, emotional, social and environmental well-being?

o   Is the practice guided by strong religious or political views?

o   Is the service offered efficient, economical, effective, appropriate, accessible and equitable?

o   Do you as a team work stressfully and reactively, or do you work in an integrative and participative way, empowering patients by building on the strengths of the team to educate and inform?

o   Do you see yourselves as instrumental in shaping and changing the future health of your patients?

o   Does the practice work closely with those sections of the community who experience the most disadvantage? Is the way you educate, inform and reach your population of paramount importance?

Set out your present standards and what you are working towards. Identify if you work comfortably with any local stakeholders, and note how the practice applies local NSFs and clinical governance targets.

Note the local NSF and clinical governance targets, then set realistic targets for yourselves.

GPs can improve health, and have a big part to play in health promotion if they:

• have adequate funding
• plan long term
• are willing to co-ordinate services
• recognise the barriers to health promotion
• educate
• research, evaluate and monitor.[1]

Annual consultation data

• Outline here how many patients the practice sees every day/month/year, divided into booked and unbooked appointments.
• State the average consultation rate per patient.
• Consult national, local or regional sources for morbidity data. Calculate, for example, how many of these contacts are estimated to be stress related (national figures suggest 23% of all episodes), how many will be related to respiratory disease (7.5% of all episodes) and so on. Use the data as a comparison to your own practice. Set out your own profile, and state your aims and objectives for each group of patients.

For an example of a practice health needs report, *see* the website.

Continue with similar profiles for all your targeted areas, for example: cancer, mental health, teenage pregnancy.

Note your current management arrangements for health needs assessment, and any resource implications.

Management team:

- GP responsible for clinical development
- practice manager – initiating, liaising, co-ordinating and reporting
- nurses – audit, clinical management and overseeing project
- X and Y – computer management.

Staffing implications:

- Auxillary nursing assistant – 0.5 to free current G grade for planning and audit activities
- VDU operator – 25 hours per week.

- Consider staff re-deployment to increase data input responsibilities.
- Encourage GPs to use computer not medical records for day to day work and clinical summaries.
- Note current and future audit activity. Note any plans that you may have in place to reach your target population. How do you plan to reach non-attenders? Will you use opportunistic screening?

Training and communication

Note how you plan to involve the whole clinical and administrative team in ensuring that lines of communication between the team are upheld, avoiding duplication of effort and cost. Review any clinical training needs and assess skills required. Note how you will audit your patients' satisfaction after the system is in place. Describe any promotional work the practice plans, e.g. to involve health visitors and practice nurses in educating patients.

⟹ **For the whole team**

Is your practice ready to achieve health gain?

○ Is your practice incorporating NSFs into practice working? Do you work to improve access to services for high risk patients?
○ Do you develop educative approaches to modify risky life-style behaviour?
○ Do you, or the practice and community nurses, use protocols?
○ Can you easily identify high risk groups? What are they?
○ Is income generation your first consideration?

Are you clear about the pros and cons of screening? Make a list here:

PROS

CONS

Government health objectives have not changed radically over the last few years. Are you aware of the most current concerns? Note them in the box overleaf.

Have you considered:

- partnership with social care
- confronting the causes of ill-health (poverty, deprivation and social exclusion)
- responding more positively to patient need?

Nursing

By 2004 we will be looking at a considerably extended role for nurses. There will be 1000 nurse consultants and over half of all nurses will be able to prescribe medicines. Practices are already preparing for the future by introducing skill mix reviews, with an outcome to save money and improve efficiency by sharing skills across practice and geographical boundaries.

Describe your current nursing structure:

- hours worked and grades
- nurse-led protocols
- nurse-led audits
- qualifications and training needs
- funding
- meeting times
- clinical and nursing issues
- NHS Plan and developments.

For an example text, *see* the website.

Nurse administration

○   Who orders and monitors vaccines?
○   Who is responsible for clinical stock control and clinical waste?
○   Who is responsible for clinical computer input?
○   Can this be developed or devolved across the whole team?
○   Is computer training required?

 ***Computer training is often free when new systems are implemented.
Make sure the whole team makes use of this.***

Nurse management

 ***Practice nurses need to see the practice managed, with themselves
managed within it. A structure which decides who is responsible
managerially and clinically is essential.***

Practice nurses are often responsible for managing nursing staff and needs,
and are often very well respected by partners and patients. Nurses clearly value
the confidence practices have in them to act autonomously. Like practice
managers, most of their thinking and development work is done in their own
time, which is unfair and unacceptable given they are generally not partners
in the business. A useful recommendation is for one doctor to manage
clinically and the practice manager to deal with personnel management.

Future nursing plans

Section 9.5 of the NHS Plan itemises how NHS employers will be required to
empower appropriately qualified nurses, midwives and therapists to
undertake a wider range of clinical tasks. Practices now need to consider how
they can plan to implement this. Many practices are in need of additional
nursing hours, to mop up the bloods, dressings and immunisations work.

 ***Practices must consider investing in an additional partner before
considering how much and what clinical work they can delegate to
the nursing staff.***

Chart what you see as the key roles for your nurses. For an example template, *see*
the website.

Include clinical targets in with your business plan overall, as they tie in with the clinical governance, training and development agenda, which in turn is part of the risk management programme.[1]

 Training is very often neglected in general practice. Training may be allocated, but practices rarely have a training and development policy for themselves or their staff.

Now is the time to act, so that the latest government targets will be met. *See* Chapter 15.

PMS

A PMS pilot is much more flexible than the national GMS contract and is suitable for anyone wishing to:

- better target the needs of a particular group of patients
- expand the range of primary care offered
- develop new arrangements/organisations for the delivery of services
- provide more flexible employment options for GPs
- give other primary care professionals greater career scope and opportunities
- expand practice capacity without extending the partnership
- streamline their contractual arrangements
- develop better human resource management systems
- develop enhanced financial management and accountability frameworks
- improve service access for their patients
- reduce the bureaucracy involved in administering the Red Book
- address local recruitment and retention problems
- improve the equity of GMS resource allocation.

A PMS contract can be formed from:

- a single practice
- a group of practices
- a whole PCG.

PMS contracts may be either:

- PMS: provision of those services which patients could normally expect to receive from any GP, e.g. GMS
- PMS+: provision of a wider range of services over and beyond that normally provided as GMS, such as non-core services or elements of hospital and community health services.

PMS principles

PMS:

- rewards quality not quantity
- adopts accepted national clinical standards
- accounts for local Health Improvement Programmes (HImPs)
- accepts a clinical governance structure
- hopes to empower local services to change
- should be developed in partnership with all stakeholders
- should ensure seamless and integrated care.

Some advantages of PMS

- PMS contracts are one way of tackling concerns about fraud.
- PMS encourages GPs to maximise and maintain their income.
- PMS contracts set minimum standards around accessibility, staffing, clinical governance and accountability.
- Large list size practices may be reluctant to increase partnership size. PMS flexibility allows practices to receive growth monies not taken up for extra partners, to develop salaried doctor and nurse practitioner posts, increasing career opportunities and satisfaction.
- Open access nurse triage is made possible.
- Allows for enhanced GMS clinics to develop in CHD, cancer, mental health, accidents, asthma, child health and ante-natal care.
- Outreach work with other agencies can be rewarded, e.g. voluntary sector and counselling services.
- Can employ community nurses directly.
- Traditional model of independent contractor status, with its financial and managerial responsibilities, together with the 24-hour responsibility for patient care, is a major contributor to stress and a significant barrier to recruitment.
- Will aid move to Trust status.
- Patients will benefit from practices working together.
- Return of flexibility for local innovation, reduced since the end of fundholding.
- PMS+ schemes will bring further benefits to patients as services transfer from secondary care.
- GPs benefit from flexible work patterns, steady cash flow, reduction in bureaucracy.
- PMS practices will automatically qualify for higher payments invested in the NHS over the next few years.

- GPs negotiate own salary and terms of service.
- Improves the equity of GMS resource usage – through improving services to deprived areas, for example.

Towards PMS: project planning/goal setting

Practices taking part in pilots could reasonably expect support from their health authority and PCG and could anticipate them to:

- carry out a full risk assessment of the practice
- agree topics of clinical audit
- produce a practice development plan pro forma.

An example of these requirements is on the website.

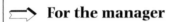 **For the manager**

As part of your project planning, you need to consider the following.

Could you answer these questions about your local community? Do you think these questions are important for your practice?

What percentage of your population have households:

- ○ where there are lone parents
- ○ where there are three or more children
- ○ where the children stay on at school after 16 years of age
- ○ where the children have been permanently excluded from school
- ○ who are in receipt of income support?

What is the standard mortality rate in your area for:

- ○ heart disease
- ○ stroke
- ○ cancer
- ○ suicides?

- ○ What is the local accident rate?
- ○ Where did the accidents occur?
- ○ Which group is most commonly hospitalised due to injury or falls?
- ○ What is the teenage pregnancy rate?
- ○ How many mothers breastfeed longer than six weeks?
- ○ How many are on the child protection register?
- ○ How many children have sound teeth?
- ○ What are the biggest fears of the population around you – Drugs? Lack of discipline? Stress? Safety? Homelessness? Business failure? Poverty? Danger of attack?

Practices which want to develop need to begin to collect data on:

- standardised mortality rates
- hospitalisation rates
- their community needs and desires

across the following health based indicators:

- heart disease, stroke and cancer
- teenage pregnancy
- accidents
- child health
- mental health.

For an example practice project plan, *see* the website.

What are the risks of PMS to your practice?

Risk	Probability	Impact
No other single-handed GP comes forward to join with us	High	High
Rest of practice don't support	Medium	High
LMC don't support	Medium	Low

Risks to anticipate

Pensions risk	Low	High
No time	Medium	High
Threat of staff duplication	High	High
No real financial gain	High	High

Reference

1   Adapted from Jacobson B, Smith A and Whitehead M (1991) *The Nation's Health: a strategy for the 1990s.* King Edward's Hospital Fund for London, London.

Further information

For more information about PMS and specialist GP schemes, contact:

NHS Alliance: www.nhsalliance.org

Retford Hospital
North Road
Retford
Nottingham
DN22 7XF

Tel: 01777 869080

The Service Development Manager
Bradford South and West PCT
Queensbury Health Centre
Russell Road
Bradford
BD13 2AG

Tel: 01274 321800

NHS Response line: 0541 555455

CHAPTER 4

Marketing and finance

Before we consider the marketing and financial aspects of the business plan, it is important to examine the practice's relationships with the outside world.

Professional relationships

Practices have many difficult relationships to maintain. Their relationship with their leaseholders is not always easy. Practices often have an uneasy relationship with their health authority or PCG/T.

This part of the business plan looks at the practice relationships with the outside world, how they view these relationships, and how these relationships impact on the health of the practice.

⇒ **For the doctors and manager**

Consider these external relationships. Mark off on a scale of 1–10 how you view the relationship:

- PCG/T
- health authority
- other local practices
- secondary care colleagues
- solicitor
- landlords
- insurance company
- the accountant
- the bank
- the Inland Revenue

- unions and professional bodies
- social care.

Even if individual relationships are good, GPs often feel constrained by the need to prove their need for more resources where they feel the need is justified. This sense has increased with what many see as a further layer of unnecessary bureaucracy with the new PCG/Ts. Practices need to balance these constraints and reconcile their current need for independent practice against dependence on the NHS as a whole. The government recognises this uneasy relationship, and the pressures on GPs to maintain a profitable small business whilst caring for patients in the best possible way. It is worth remembering that as GPs you have the power and authority to action change as you work at the 'coal face', directly influencing patient care. Managers are more distant from patient activity.

GPs no longer rely entirely on capitation and item of service payments, and gradually over the years different reward schemes have emerged to encourage a quality service. Target payments were introduced, then additional payments for additional services such as health promotion and minor operation clinics. GPs are still in the enviable position of receiving heavy subsidies (for staff, premises and equipment) for what is still a private business. However, these reimbursement levels have been eroded. The new recommendation, giving a PMS or salaried option, is going to take the majority of GPs out of independent contractor status into a purchaser/provider service, with quality demands set by outside external agencies.

It is therefore imperative that GPs who want to develop their business develop their external relationships too, as they will become increasingly dependent on those purchasing their service. Relationships with the bank and accountant will be less important as more and more GPs opt for a salaried contract. GPs wishing to take up a PMS option, which will look increasingly attractive, will need to reconsider their financial future carefully, especially older GPs who need to protect their pensions and those partnerships who have bought their own premises.

Relationships with secondary and social care colleagues are sometimes constrained: there are always tensions where services are led and managed externally without communication with primary care and GPs are reluctant to take on additional care without additional funding if the service is transferred. Consultant colleagues are sometimes reluctant to relinquish their responsibilities unless they are assured their GP colleagues are running accredited programmes of care for patients. Not all GPs are motivated to take on this additional work, and some are motivated but unable to due to lack of staff, skills or premises. GPs complain about variations in levels of service provision and quality from different providers. Everyone complains about funding.

> ⟹ **For the doctors**

What are the local secondary and social care led services you are most worried about?

Think of some solutions to problems.

What about:

- ○ multi-disciplinary education and working
- ○ setting up local specialist clinics run by GPs
- ○ using more specialist nurses as facilitators to liaise between the two sectors
- ○ giving all GPs the financial incentive to run their own accredited programmes of care?

Marketing

Position and policy dictate where practices trade and advertise: many still consider GP advertising to be unprofessional – it is certainly usually unnecessary. Most practices use their practice leaflets, charters and reputations to carry their businesses successfully, and it is still unusual to see a practice advertise for business. It is possible to discreetly inform the public of your 'unique selling point' using a practice leaflet, but more aggressive advertising may be necessary if you run a private business, for example a travel clinic, where you may have a licence to sell products. You then need to be aware of pricing tactics, i.e. selling at a price that will make a decent profit without limiting the product appeal. When selling, it is worth remembering one sales adage: the more expensive a product is, the more sought after it will be. However, this usually only applies if the product is unique; if mosquito nets and jungle spray are selling at a nearby chemist at half the price, this does not apply.

If you are selling on products you need to consider the following.

○   What is your product's life?
○   Has the product been market tested?
○   Who are your major suppliers?
○   Are you selling the right products:
  –   in the right place
  –   at the right time
  –   at the right price?
○   Are you promoting in the right way?
○   Are you promoting to the right people?

To be successful at promoting your goods, you need to produce a mini-business plan where you:

•   analyse opportunities (who needs our products – what are our strengths and our customer needs?)
•   select realistic targets and objectives
•   define roles
•   provide a sense of purpose for the business
•   develop strategy
•   prepare a SWOT analysis
•   develop tactics to beat the opposition
•   draw up a plan according to resources held
•   implement and control – make it happen.

Your marketing plan could address:

- financial targets and anticipated turnover, controls and budgets
- a product plan: to improve or develop existing products
- a pricing plan: trends, competitors and discounts
- market information: market and customer research and competitors
- a sales plan
- a promotional plan: use of media, sponsorship and direct marketing
- structure/staffing: training, incentives and organisation.

Ask customers regularly:

- what they think of existing products
- what improvements or additions they would like to see
- what unfulfilled needs they have
- about value for money.

 Note for new practices.

Allow time for marketing, advertising, promoting, and generating new business. Flyers work, but advertising generally is seen as tacky and non-productive. Be prepared to self-promote a new practice when networking. Repeat businesses is best, and recommendations to friends and family from existing, and satisfied, patients. Aim to provide a quality service, without concern initially for the list size.

Life for the single-handed practice is now limited: keep abreast of government plans and look to see how you could join up with other single-handed practices locally and with whom.

Note how the practice promotes itself in the business plan

Example

The practice uses its practice leaflets and reputation to carry its business successfully. Business is thriving and in fact we are to some extent the victim of our own success with more new patients registering than we can manage. It will not be necessary to use more aggressive advertising.

While general practice is still a private business, practices may choose to advertise, but some see this as tacky. Price and position dictate where one trades and advertises: GPs would be wise to choose local, up-market magazines or periodicals.

> ⟹ **For the manager**

Which ones would you choose?

1

2

3

Advertising

The current (2001) GMC advertising guidelines require that information must:

- be factual
- be verifiable
- conform to law
- conform to guidance published by the Advertising Standards Authority
- be easily understood: worded simply, in plain English.

It must not:

- make claims about the quality of services
- compare with services provided by colleagues
- put pressure on people to use a service
- offer guarantees of cures
- exploit vulnerable patients.

Licensing and legalities

Business relationships

Practices need to maintain good relationships with close professional groups. Professional advice may need to be sought from a solicitor, who can advise on:

- partnership law
- premises buying and development
- lease restrictions if you are using your own premises to work from
- local by-laws that prevent practice
- partnership agreements
- local trading restrictions and environmental health regulations.

If you are selling on goods (e.g. a travel clinic) you may need contractual advice on:

- taking over a franchise
- trading laws: goods must live up to the claims made for them, and follow safety standards
- standards and patents
- copyright
- complying with business name law
- rental licences.

Note the relationships with the accountant and bank. Is the practice a good credit risk with:

- ○ good security
- ○ ability to meet repayments
- ○ clear credit references
- ○ assets available as security?

Insurance

What sort of insurances should the practice and partnership consider?

Which of the following must you have, and which are optional? What are they for?

o   Personal liability.
o   Contents.
o   Premises.
o   Building.
o   Equipment.
o   Life or term insurance.
o   Sickness.
o   Redundancy.
o   Critical illness.
o   Health protection.

Bank

- You may need a second account as a small business, or an overdraft facility. If so, talk to the small business advisor.
- Cultivate a relationship with the bank manager. They want security, ability to meet repayments, clear credit references and to have assets available as security.
- Consider a Business Development Loan or Business Reserve Account for surplus cash. Discuss life assurance, savings and pensions planning.
- Many banks now advertise offering specific advice to GP or healthcare customers. As they have built up a bank of specialist knowledge, consider changing your account to one of these.

Other contacts

Does the practice network widely, or are individuals active in their professional societies, e.g. AMSPAR, Institute of Management or the Institute of Health Service Managers?

Working in partnership

 If the GPs work in partnership with each other, each partner is jointly liable for each other's debts. Again, this is a huge risk to take without a partnership agreement drawn up by a solicitor.

Employing

Many practices now utilise the services of counsellors or complementary practitioners to work within the practice. If the practice *employs* someone else, then they would need to be either:

- self-employed, with a 'contract for services', or
- working under PAYE, with a 'contract of service'.

If they work under PAYE, they are an employee, and as an employer you are responsible for PAYE and need to set up a contract of employment, provide a job description and register your member of staff with the Inland Revenue. If, however, the person is self-employed, you will need:

- their schedule D reference number
- to confirm with the DSS their self-employed status, class 2 NI
- to request regular invoices
- to check they have a professional indemnity insurance policy
- to find out if they are providing their own equipment and materials
- to check their qualifications and experience
- to check if their work is regularly supervised
- to make clear that you do not pay sick or holiday pay
- to make clear that the self-employed person is responsible for their own training, development and supervision costs.

Finance

Currently, about 10% of GPs in the UK are employed, with the number rising year on year. The remaining 90% prefer to continue to work as independent self-employed contractors. Financial concerns for this latter group are complex and need managing carefully. The majority of practices employ external accountants who carry the responsibility for reporting on the financial situation. However, practice managers need to control the finances on a daily basis, reporting to both the partners and the accountants. Managers need to understand:

- how cash is pumped around the business
- where the pressure points are
- where surplus cash can be drained off.

Work closely with your accountants – the success of the accounting function depends on its relationship with users.

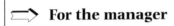 **For the manager**

○ Do you understand what is being produced by the accountant?
○ Do you understand why it is being produced?
○ Do you understand the jargon? Some terms – 'profit', 'loss', 'value' and 'cost' do not have common, widely accepted definitions. Check these terms out with your accountant.

Companies are obliged by law to prepare a set of financial statements each year. It is essential for managers to know how they are prepared and what they disclose.

What are the following? Are you familiar with, and can you interpret:

○ the profit and loss account?

This is a measure of the operating performance of a business over a given period of time.

○ the balance sheet?

This is a statement of what it owns (assets) and what it owes (liabilities) at a particular time, usually the last day of the financial year.

Management accounting

This is what you will have the most exposure to as a manager. It is here that financial information is analysed and disseminated in a user friendly form as a basis for decision making. Management accounting information is provided on a regular basis, usually monthly or quarterly. This will involve:

* keeping track of transactions and the subsequent impact on the wealth of the business:
  – recording the results
  – measuring the consequences
  – projecting the effect
* the planning and control of essential functions, tracking performance to plan:
  – collecting cash
  – paying suppliers
  – paying wages
  – co-ordinating and monitoring budgets
* providing sufficient information for others to determine future activities
* checking performance against prior targets.

Budgetary control

Budgets help make an organisation run more smoothly and profitably. Anyone who influences cost should be given a budget against which to measure actual expense. Budget holders must exist within a well defined structure to avoid overlap of responsibilities.

 General practices continually put their business at risk by not planning ahead financially.

In general practice, a common problem is the need to improve resource management and develop appropriate management systems. Practices need to develop robust financial control systems as a matter of urgency. The most common fault is that practices do not set up budgets, or systems to predict their cash flow.

Successful budgeting depends on:

- co-operation and communication between budget holders
- realistic and achievable targets against which to measure expenditure
- consistent objectives
- constructive, not punitive feedback
- well designed and easily read budget reports
- timely, detailed and accurate reporting
- regular meetings
- flexible budgeting which allows for changes in business activity
- classifying costs as fixed or variable
- analysing variance – the difference between actual costs and budget.

 For the doctors and manager

What do you see as the advantage of budgets?

Some advantages of budgets

- The organisation's objectives are clearly defined in financial terms.
- Key actions are highlighted.
- Ways of measuring performance can be clearly identified.
- Budgets give an overview of the entire organisation's activities.
- Early warning of problems is given so corrective action may be initiated.
- Correctly performed, the budgeting process can be a positive motivating experience.

What are the disadvantages?

Some disadvantages of budgets
- They are time consuming to prepare and review.
- Budgets may constrain individuals if imposed.

Describe what happens currently in your practice. Who is responsible for finance, who monitors, who controls?

For an example, *see* the website.

 **For the partners**

Do you put monies aside for:

○ locum cover
○ staff holiday cover
○ partnership personal tax liability
○ additional pension cover
○ equipment and decorating

in an interest bearing account? If not, why not? Remember you are still self-employed!

Most practices use a simple debit and credit system which is reconciled monthly and uses main headings such as equipment, locum expenses, petty cash, etc. Within this, the payroll is run with or without external assistance and GMS items of service and private payments (maternity, immunisations, cremations, PMRs, etc.) are logged but not routinely analysed. Partnership tax is usually best dealt with directly by external accountants, but a good internal accountant will take the accounts up to trial balance level and advise on tax issues.

For an example of a credit/debit system (the cash book), *see* the website.

 The strategic practice audits and analyses income and expenditure at least quarterly.

A good quality financial software package such as Quicken or SAGE can be used for this, as it produces good graphic displays on reporting. Any trust-worthy member of staff competent with the computer could be trained to produce the reports for the manager to analyse and present a quarterly finance paper to the partners.

To summarise: practices must build in more robust financial controls.

- One partner should take responsibility for requesting and analysing the practice finances. This partner can take responsibility for all financial decisions and take the information required to the partnership meetings.
- Practices should audit and analyse income and expenditure at least quarterly.
- The practice should set up an interest bearing account and put aside monies (5–10%) for locum cover, staff holiday cover payments, their personal tax liability, equipment and decorating.
- The practice should devolve a cash flow forecasting system for the practice accounts.
- The manager should take strategic responsibility for setting up systems to enable these financial controls to be put in place.

For an example of annual cash flow forecast, *see* the website.

Many practices make a conscious decision to run a small overdraft on their current accounts. This is not necessarily bad practice, if the decision is conscious and the account meticulously monitored. If this is the case, it may be an idea to implement a plan to systematically reduce the overdraft – set yourself a target and reduce it by £x per month over y period.

Example of applying financial controls

Annual spending summary plan
A cash flow forecast is a first step towards understanding the practice finances. Separate fixed and variable income and expenditure.

Fixed expenditure
- Cleaning, laundry, etc.
- Rent, mortgage, car park, etc.
- Utilities (gas, electricity, water, telephone, business tax, etc.). Pay by direct debit and fix the monthly payment.
- Postage, stationery, etc.
- Catering.
- Petty cash.
- Maintenance charges.

Variable expenditure
- Capital costs: equipment, computer, hard and software and faxes.
- Staff holiday cover.
- Meeting costs.

Cost the GPs' time per hour by looking at their average annual drawings, divided by 52 (for the weeks of the year), divided again by the hours of an average working week. This will give you a working cost. Some GPs prefer to use the current GMS guidelines of their hourly worth – currently around £140 per hour. Using this as a guideline, one can calculate the cost to the practice of their four doctors and manager attending a half-hour meeting.

Meeting costs	Monthly cost	Annual cost
Business planning meetings		
Needs assessment meetings		
Whole practice meetings		
Partnership meetings		
Prescribing reviews		
Locum payments		
Other meetings		
Totals		

For an example of staff costs (to include pensions and NIC), *see* the website.

 **For the partners and manager**

For most doctors, income has remained static over the last few years as a direct result of increased spending on staff, computers and rising medical defence costs. There are concerns about a lack of resources to meet the new challenges set, particularly around prescribing. Pay awards for GPs in the past few years have not been generous, so it is increasingly important to consider ways of not only increasing income, but also reducing expenditure.

⇒ **For the doctors and manager**

Think about the financial implications and increase in workload from the following initiatives:

- rising patient expectations
- new medical advances
- national service frameworks
- clinical governance
- PCG/T meetings
- IT administration
- prescribing
- new screening initiatives
- cardiac initiatives
- less waiting time for patients
- letters to patients
- NHS Direct expansion
- monitoring GP referrals
- free retirement MOTs
- new flu prescribing
- revalidation and appraisal requirements.

Add some of your own:

Can you cost them?

For some tips to reduce the bills, *see* the website.

Avoiding fraud and managing financial risk

Fraud happens every day in general practice: GPs defraud the NHS, GPs defraud each other and practice staff defraud GPs. Have you strategies in place for preventing such occurrences? What can help?

- Evidence-based practice.
- Use of policies.
- Risk reduction.
- Systematic monitoring.
- High quality healthcare delivery.
- Team work.
- Scrutiny from an informed public.
- Staff training.
- Practice performance indicators.
- Systems and structures.

 For the doctors and manager

Consider the following possibilities. What would you consider fraudulent behaviour?

- Theft from petty cash box.
- Reimbursement claim for non-existent member of staff.
- A false invoice submitted against a computer claim.
- False quotes – undercutting others – obtained for building work in exchange for a commission.
- A favoured contractor submits quotes using dummy letterheads.
- Bribery.
- A favoured taxi firm is given priority to collect patients from surgery.
- A member of staff redirects ordered office goods to own home for personal use or re-sale.
- A member of staff lies about their qualifications or experience when obtaining the job.
- A friend or relative obtains a job in the practice as a favour.
- A member of staff works with a corrupt supplier, and pays for goods not received.
- A practice manager draws in excess of their quoted salary.

Have you strategies in place for preventing such occurrences? Have you:

- anticipated the possibility
- provided fail-safe written systems

○   created firewalls between individuals and temptations
○   limited opportunities
○   created a whistle-blowing policy?

Does the practice:

○   have written documents confirming who has access to what, when and
     where
○   do regular and visible stock checks
○   immediately check, verify and record goods delivered into the practice
○   keep written records to check against
○   separate the key holder from the accounts
○   have a system for double checking the accounts
○   make sure two people are responsible for different elements of each
     procedure
○   always obtain references when appointing
○   always ask to see any relevant certificates
○   obtain all quotes in sealed envelopes
○   apply critical incident policies to non-clinical behaviour
○   keep good records of stock ordering, payments and prices
○   countersign all cheques and ordering – whatever amount check all
     cheques before signing
○   divide up management responsibilities – delegate so one person does not
     have all the control
○   make sure financial information (manual and computer) is accessible to
     more than one person
○   inspect and understand all financial returns to the health authority –
     especially staff salaries
○   have a rigorous procedure for accounting for overtime?

Does the practice run efficient stores?

•   Stock should be easily accessible.
•   Facilities and equipment should match requirements.
•   Goods should be secured against theft.
•   You should create efficient stock locator systems.

Don't assume your practice will be exempt – manage the risk.
Be alert to things going wrong!

Some warning signs

Lack of management action
If it is clear that management are not in control, it is probable they are not
planning ahead. Likely symptoms of this include:

•   lack of specific plans to solve problems
•   failure to identify market developments in advance

- hope for general recovery rather than specific action
- failure to identify the precise nature of performance failure
- policy and operations being unreasonably dominated by the personal views of a single individual – particularly the business owner
- lack of recognition of the need to identify problems and their management
- complacency or a lack of sense of urgency, despite major problems
- failure to develop remedial action plans despite eroding resources.

Failure to manage the accounting function
Likely symptoms include:

- accounts being inaccurate or lacking credibility
- bank accounts not being reconciled
- analysis of creditors and debtors not happening
- inventories not being maintained or being unreliable
- failure to operate budgetary controls
- failure to develop annual budget plans routinely
- delays in monthly reporting
- key items missing from reports
- consistent large unexplained variances from budget
- substantial delays in preparing year end accounts.

 Practices considering PMS status will need to start maximising their target income and begin developing mechanisms for identifying correct funding sources and amounts.

Practices will be asked to set out how they plan to fund the services they intend to provide. In addition, they will be asked to quantify their historic use of GMS resources – the levels of income including item of service payments received.

In general, services will be funded from a transfer of GMS non-discretionary funds, which will be based on the historic levels of GMS funding (the level of funding currently received from Red Book payments).

If practices propose to expand their services, then the funding must be clearly identified. Additional funding will come from:

- GMS discretionary monies for GMS services
- the Hospital and Community Health Services (HCHS) budget for services traditionally provided by hospitals.

Practices must begin to identify how their pilot is to be financed and from which pot. It is clear from this description that there is no more new money available for PMS development, but it is likely that, as with all new initiatives, health authorities and PCG/Ts will give every support to practices wishing to develop in this way.

Salaried or not?

Are you a:

○ locum
○ deputy
○ retainee
○ assistant
○ PMS pilot
○ salaried
○ independent contractor principal?

Is your employer:

○ the health authority
○ a PCT
○ a practice
○ a PMS pilot
○ a co-operative
○ a deputising firm
○ a commercial company?

GPs are still paid by a variety of methods all of which are complicated. Most GPs are self-employed, but about 10% are employed, and that number is rising.

Salaried

If you are salaried, you will:

• have a contract
• work set hours
• have a salary
• have paid holiday
• have paid sick leave
• pay tax on a PAYE basis.

There is a wide range of salaries on offer, but a full time assistant can usually expect to earn 75% of an average independent contractor principal, and of course would not be expected to take on additional partnership responsibilities, managerial or administrative work or out of hours work.

Check your contract before signing.

○ Does it include expenses such as subscriptions to your MDU?
○ Are you being paid sessionally or are you truly salaried?
○ Is there an out of hours commitment?
○ Compare it with a BMA model contract.

Self-employed locums have:

- no paid annual leave
- no paid study leave
- no sick pay
- no pension rights
- no employment rights.

The practice additionally saves on National Insurance, and if locums work in one place for longer than three months, the Inland Revenue regards their stay as permanent.

For further information for the beginner, *see* the website.

Check your knowledge of the jargon. Do you know what the following mean?

- drawings
- PAYE
- taxable net income
- gross earnings
- necessary expenses

- principal
- GMS
- independent contractor status
- Red Book

PART TWO

CHAPTER 5

Clinical risk

'To assure quality is to ensure that patients receive such care as is most likely to produce the optimal achievable outcome... consistent with biological circumstances... concomitant pathology... compliance with recommended treatment... minimal expense... lowest achievable risk to patient... and maximal satisfaction with process and results.'

The World Health Organisation[1]

In this section we look at ways to apply the new clinical governance agenda through risk management – identifying the tools required to manage risk within your practice. This includes:

- managing clinical risk
- managing organisational risk
- building in mechanisms to avoid mistakes made in communicating with staff, patients, or external organisations
- managing information technology
- managing the risks of organisational stagnation (through analysing the clinical needs of your client group)
- the benefits of audit in managing risk.

In the first two chapters we look at the importance of the clinical role in helping to make clinical governance a success.

'Success is not reached through concentration on profit increases. The way to success is through minimising losses.'

Anita Roddick

Clinical governance has been introduced with an aim of bringing together all of the components of good clinical practice and quality and arranging to measure and monitor them. It aims to improve patient care through achieving high standards, reflective practice and risk management as well as personal and professional development.

It has a strong resemblance to the concept of total quality management (TQM).[2] Although in the public sector Roddick's concept of profit can be removed, we could re-word this to make it applicable to general practice today: reduce risk by constantly improving the product you are offering in relation to the customer's needs.

Clinical governance incorporates:

- quality improvement activities
- the identification and management of risk
- continuing professional development.

What are the principles of clinical governance? It involves:

- co-operating and working with others
- applying the principles locally, to your practice
- focusing on improving and maintaining high standards of care
- helping you to ensure good practice
- setting clear service standards
- performing clinical audits
- ensuring evidence-based practices are carried out
- collecting records to help review performance and monitor patient care
- implementing risk management plans
- reporting adverse healthcare incidents
- setting clear performance standards for all staff
- promoting a learning environment
- valuing openness
- involving patients.

The systems embraced by clinical governance include:

- clinical audit
- risk management
- revalidation
- evidence-based clinical practice (NICE, CHI, protocols and local guidance)
- development of clinical leadership skills
- continuing education for all staff (PDP and PPDP)
- audit of consumer feedback
- accreditation.

GPs are aware of the emerging tensions between equality/choice, demand/resources, efficiency/quality and managing these tensions is crucial. As independent practitioners, there will always be a major tension between providing the very best clinical care versus the cost of that care. And practising the very best medicine at all times is impossible – the aim must always be to minimise the risk of harm.

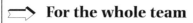 **For the whole team**

Some clinical governance terms follow. Are you familiar with these?

- Accreditation of healthcare.
- Underperformance of clinicians.
- Core values.
- Competence.
- Revalidation.
- Quality of care.
- Performance assessment frameworks.
- Performance indicators.

Quality of care

Big steps have been taken by the government to improve the quality of NHS care by introducing:

- National Service Frameworks
- the National Institute for Clinical Excellence
- the Commission for Health Improvement (CHI)
- the NHSNet.

Between them, they provide a framework that evaluates levels and types of clinical care, and makes recommendations on the best, outcome based treatments available currently. This has removed the necessity for each individual health authority or GP practice to define their own treatments, which in the past led to a postcode lottery of prescribing and care.

Many GPs have, of course, felt affronted by this, as they are well qualified to assess, diagnose and define the correct treatment for their own patients. But there is now more understanding of the need to work with finite resources, and the awareness that there is no time for every individual clinician to be a clinical specialist in every field. It has been said that each GP would need to read 90 clinical papers a day for the rest of their working life to maintain the level of knowledge gleaned at medical school. Clearly this is impossible – hence the need to make specialist knowledge clear, evidence-based and accessible. Most supporting management teams are aware of the need to involve GPs in applying the principles set by the government, hence PCG/Ts support practices in defining their own needs and solutions in relation to those set locally and nationally. All guidelines have within them room for innovation: the problem professionally seems to be not one of restriction but one of conservatism – most GPs are in fact reluctant to take up new treatments.

Pharmaceutical companies are happy to support practices who feel they need more help with developing clinical initiatives. They often have a team of skilled facilitators and trainers who can assist, offering a solutions based approach to improving healthcare. Approach one of your representatives for ideas and/or sponsorship.

What is quality?

- Value for money.
- Fitness for purpose.
- Customer satisfaction.

Here are some things that have been said about quality. Can you apply some of them to your organisation?

- Commitment and example from management.
- An approach which focuses on the customer.
- A participative environment and team work.
- An organisation in pursuit of continuous improvement.
- The organisation exists to meet the needs of the patient not itself.

Performance assessment framework

 For the whole team

Does your practice provide care that is:

- **accessible** (no physical, cultural or linguistic barriers, timely)
- **appropriate** (conforms to legislation, research based, meets needs of the population)
- **effective** (promotes health and recovery, research based, NSF guidelines followed)
- **efficient** (best use of resources, skills, money, people, buildings, equipment)
- **equitable** (respectful to all, service provided on basis of need not personal characteristics)
- **relevant** (responsive to the population served, sufficient, balanced, no gaps)
- **acceptable** (meets the cultural and religious expectations of the users)
- **knowledge based** (sound and accurate information supporting decision making)
- **accountable** (principally and financially, care is outcome based)
- **integrative** (involves other agencies)?

Total Quality Management (TQM) does not supplant traditional approaches, it simply provides the tools with which traditional medical knowledge can be made to work better.

- It is concerned with achieving value for money and using resources effectively.
- It gives workers more opportunity to contribute to the development of services.
- It changes the culture of an organisation to achieve tangible benefits for everyone.
- It fails when the leaders are uncommitted or suppress desires for improvement.
- It aims not just to satisfy the needs of the patient but to delight them.
- It aims for continuous improvement not just front of house superficialities.
- It harnesses conflict and focuses on improving processes.
- It seeks to reduce inter-professional wrangling.
- It does not just improve numbers but also services.
- It is involved with improvement not punishment – if your patients require more expensive care because they are older and more fragile this is a fine and defensible position.

⟹ **For the clinicians**

What do you see as the advantages and disadvantages of clinical governance?

+   –

Who in your practice is responsible for clinical governance?

Who is the clinical lead on this in your PCG/T?

continued overleaf

> **NSFs: the five service frameworks produced so far cover between them around half of the total NHS spend, and account for the highest mortality rates. Can you name them?**
>
> **There are six components in the NSF performance assessment framework. What are they?**

The five service frameworks produced so far are: mental health, coronary heart disease, the National Cancer Plan, older people's services and diabetes.

The six components of the NSF performance assessment framework are: health improvement, fair access, efficiency, effective delivery of appropriate care, user/carer experience and health outcomes.

Is all your practice evidence-based?

The Department of Health[3] adapted Roth and Fonagy's principles applied to psychotherapy research and produced a four-step model for improved patient care. This model can be used reliably for any service provision.

Commission systematic research reviews

⇓

Secure professional consensus

⇓

Implement evidence-based practice

⇓

Benchmark service outcomes

⇓

Improved patient care[4]

NICE

What does NICE actually do?

NICE appraises what are considered to be the best interventions and treatments and produces guidelines to ensure a faster, more uniform, uptake of treatments which work best for patients.

○ How do you access NICE guidelines? What is the mechanism for you to become involved in prioritising and actioning NICE recommendations in your area?

NICE is one strand of clinical governance. The team offers authoritative guidance on the highest standards of care. It aims to improve the nature and completeness of data held in general practice through:

- appraising technology
- developing clinical care programmes
- promoting monitoring of clinical performance through
  - audit
  - referral protocols
  - procedural manuals
  - nursing benchmarks
  - disease management protocols
  - integrated care pathways
  - clinical guidelines that are: multi-disciplinary, formally evidenced, clinical and cost effective, applicable to the majority.

NSFs

NSFs aim to make research answer the questions GPs ask.

NSFs establish models of treatment and care based on evidence of best practice. They look for uniformity of treatment to a minimum standard, and consistency across major care areas. They provide a treatment framework for a particular disorder or group of diseases. They aim to address:

- healthcare improvements
- inequalities of access
- differences of outlook
- differences of outcome
- differences in quality of care
- postcode rationing.

Principles of NSFs

NSFs cover:

- the programme of care from primary through to tertiary and secondary care
- primary/secondary care prevention, rehabilitation
- parity: to lift the bottom 40% into parity
- shorter waiting lists
- technical change, e.g. NHS Direct/direct booking systems
- faster, more convenient access
- milestones that can be developed over 4–6 years
- setting standards/benchmarks
- referral advice
- collaboration with relevant professional bodies
- 80% of the population
- clinical risk management – if guidelines are not adhered to, there will be MDU implications
- links with NHS Research and Development centre.

Using NSFs in practice: using your computer to construct a coronary heart disease (CHD) register

By now, most practices will be familiar with the CHD NSF, one of the first to be set up following research which demonstrated that CHD was one of the most poorly managed chronic diseases in primary care. This NSF requires a CHD register to be in use by April 2001, and the first audit to be completed two years later. The clinical audit criteria and standards can be found within the CHD NSF, and most PCG/T clinical governance groups are working at disseminating the information and encouraging and supporting practices to meet the NSF criteria. Contact your PCG/T clinical governance lead if in doubt.

For more information on the NSF for CHD, *see* the website.

Preventing CHD

- Who within the practice is going to manage this process?
- Who will assess, give advice and prescribe?
- Who will set up and manage the recall process?
- Who will manage the audit process?
- How, specifically, are you going to set up primary prevention measures for those at risk?

Are you aware of the key investigations and treatment in:

○ stable angina
○ heart failure?

Some solutions

- Most practices have up to date prescribing data on their system – if a patient is prescribed a drug there should be a reason for them taking the drug – this can be coded.
- Set up your computer system so you can only access the next field when the previous one is complete.
- If you are computer-phobic, create a stamp for medical records for opportunistic consultation.
- See if your PCG can produce, or a drug company sponsor the production of, hand held cards for patients with CHD which educate and inform them of the recall procedure for your practice.
- Train up your admin staff:
    - to highlight diagnoses on hospital letters
    - to input new registration and hospital letter information on the computer
    - to audit.
- Consider investing in a standard, accredited programme to collect the data such as MIQUEST (*see* Chapter 8).

The Coronary Heart Disease NSF is the first one to be introduced into general practice universally. A similar process will be adopted for the other NSFs as they emerge. Think of some of the ways your practice can absorb the workload without additional resources.

Commission for Health Improvement (CHI)

Both CHI organisationally and the GMC, individually, seek to ensure the quality of clinical practice and services for patients, whilst continuously driving forward a concept of development, continued improvement, encouraging and sharing best practice. CHI aims to provide a framework for NHS institutions to be accountable for their actions. Public confidence has been rocked in the wake of Bristol, Alder Hey and Dr Shipman. CHI has been set up by the government to address such dangerous incidents and variations in performance. It aims, like the NSFs and NICE guidelines, to co-ordinate risk management, reinforce clinical audit, and address adverse incidents. It aims, overall, for a reduction in morbidity and mortality in the NHS institutions it inspects.

CHI principles

To be:

- patient centred
- independent and fair
- developmental/active learning
- evidence-based
- open and approachable
- focused on patient care not cost.

CHI's roles are to:

- investigate, review, evaluate, and implement:
  - CG reviews
  - NSF studies
  - NICE guidelines
- investigate serious failures
- give advice and information to GPs.

CHI operates on four levels:

- corporate
- patients
- clinical and teams
- peer review.

All these systems have been set up with an aim to support the NHS through a difficult time, where a change in culture has meant doctors are no longer exempt from public criticism.

Revalidation

'Do you know your PDP and PPDP from your PID?'

Dr Paul Moore

The government is setting up additional rapid and robust mechanisms for dealing with poor and underperforming doctors. The GMC's new revalidation programme means that:

- clinical audit is compulsory
- all doctors employed or under contract are required to participate in annual appraisal

- non-principals and locums are placed on a local register and are required to report how they contribute to practices in which they work
- all doctors working in primary care are subject to clinical governance arrangements
- a mandatory scheme for reporting significant healthcare events is being developed: there will be a single database for analysing and sharing lessons learned from incidents and near misses
- GPs are to keep personal portfolios demonstrating their professional and educational development.

This replaces the old mechanism of PGEAs, and there is no fixed amount of time attached to the process; the learning will occur in and out of the consultation room and it is expected that GPs will make any learning and recording integral to their working day. However, at least initially, some PCG/Ts are offering help and support through MAAG facilitation, learning sets, etc.

It is understood that GPs will probably be assessed in alphabetical order, and it will be a rolling five-year programme. The assessment will be carried out by a local revalidation group consisting of, most probably:

- a locally elected GP
- a lay person
- one PCG or health authority person, possibly a medical director
- one educationalist, who could also be a GP.

If the group are concerned about failing performance, they will have the authority to refer the individual to the GMC with a recommendation that s/he be revalidated.

The business of reviewing, discussing and ensuring the safety of an individual doctor's performance remains contentious and presents a unique challenge. None of us wants to think of doctors as being anything other than perfect in their knowledge, skills, and ability to make decisions. Doctors' decisions have profound effects on people's lives, so when a doctor performs to a poor standard, something needs to be done. The real challenge lies in creating a system which acknowledges and rewards progress and achievement, whilst simultaneously identifying and supporting those whose performance has deteriorated.

The new system aims to capture and support those doctors who:

- have failed to keep up to date
- are discourteous to patients
- work badly with colleagues
- make poor or dangerous clinical decisions.

It is now more widely accepted that clinicians' performance must be monitored, reviewed and improved continuously throughout a career, in the same way that other professions are – teachers, nurses and independent financial advisors.

Personal Development Plans (PDPs)

Each GP is to carry a personal folder, confidential to them, that should contain:

- a description of current practice
- a description of chosen fields of work or specialties, and time appropor-tioned to this
- personal profiles demonstrating continuing educational and professional development
- demonstrations of good clinical care, good relationships with patients and colleagues
- audit results
- appraisal
- complaints
- compliments
- any significant events (including critical incidents).

GMC members have also recently agreed these revalidation folders could include:

- details of criminal convictions
- disciplinary hearings
- any breaks in registration that occurred during the revalidation period
- any conditions placed on the registration by the GMC, any erasure or suspensions.

A PDP should be a document that encompasses the context and culture of your working environment as well as the skills and knowledge relating to your post. It should:

- identify noted weaknesses in knowledge, skills, attitudes
- identify how, and what, you have learned from your mistakes
- note changes in your role or responsibilities which create new learning opportunities
- prioritise your learning needs and set outcomes
- set goals and describe how these will be achieved over a set period of time
- justify your selection of these goals
- describe how you plan to evaluate your outcomes.

> ⟹ **For the doctors**

Do you:

- use a range of methods to identify your learning needs
- make certain you are open to new ideas
- continue your professional development
- know your role
- learn from experience
- listen actively
- respond fairly to assessments of your practice
- take advantage of opportunities to learn on the job
- take part in staff training programmes
- keep up to date
- make suggestions for improvement in your practice?

 GPs need not just academic competence but operational competence.

Core values

What makes a good doctor? Clearly good GPs cannot be measured solely by statistics. One of the measuring tools that the GPC, GMC and RCGP may be looking at is a competence assessment scheme. Competence based assessment is big in the USA, and is spreading this way. The idea is not just to explore academic competence but operational competence. Recent research[5] has identified some key competence criteria, qualities found in GPs most commonly mentioned in recommendation made by other GPs looking for medical care for their own family or friends:

- empathy and sensitivity
- team involvement
- personal organisation and administrative skills
- stress-coping mechanisms
- communication skills
- legal, ethical and political awareness
- personal attributes
- professional integrity
- conceptual thinking
- job's relationship to society and family
- personal development
- clinical knowledge
- managing others
- learning and development.

It is worth thinking how useful these competencies are in running a business centred around patient care, and also considering the import of these qualities when peer assessing for revalidation.[5]

What are learning needs?

What range of methods do you use to identify your learning needs? How do you prioritise your training needs? Can you demonstrate that you:

- gain feedback from colleagues
- appraise yourself and your attitudes, knowledge, awareness of health politics and skills
- conduct audit or research
- compare your performance with others
- observe your work role and environment
- read and reflect
- take part in any educational appraisal or mentoring scheme
- analyse patient contacts through case review
- video tape consultations
- analyse prescribing or practice activity data
- undergo objective testing
- attend educational meetings or training programmes?

Patients' Unmet Needs (PUNs)

Looking at PUNs may be a good way of identifying your learning needs, as if you do not meet your patient's needs this may be due to your lack of knowledge or skill – thus identifying the Doctors' Unmet Needs (DUNs). This can be done through transcribing, or analysing, difficult and unsatisfactory consultations, and identifying where you went wrong – at what point did the communication between you break down?

If this information is shared, it helps a team learn, and you build up a profile of the knowledge and skills possessed by that team.

Significant Events Analysis (SEAs)

Have you ever had examples of these events in your surgery:

- a missed diagnosis
- an unexpected and unnecessary death
- the theft of a script pad
- staff upset by behaviour of the doctor or manager
- a patient highlighting poor service delivery
- a patient behaving violently

- o   a confidential message left on the wrong answerphone
- o   payment claims missed
- o   a burglary
- o   a computer crash
- o   a row with a patient
- o   a missed visit?

It is not easy to have our deficiencies exposed by our practice colleagues, patients or staff, but without acknowledging that mistakes can be made no learning, or personal development, occurs. Significant events can be examples of when things go right as well as wrong, and again, group (practice, not just doctor) discussion and analysis enables whole team learning and change to occur.

Again you can ask yourself:

- o   What are the facts here?
- o   What went well?
- o   What went badly?
- o   How could I improve?
- o   What action should be taken?
- o   How should the event be recorded?

Appraisals for GPs

'Appraisal is to the individual professional as clinical governance is to organisations and services.'

'This is the first time in 25 years of medicine, that anyone has asked me if I am happy in my job.'[6]

The traditional approach to appraisal has been hierarchical – manager appraising subordinate. The ethos and culture of medicine makes peer appraisal difficult, but not impossible. The purpose of appraisal is not to undertake a disciplinary interview, but to jointly:

- •   assess training and development needs
- •   help improve current performance
- •   review past performance – spotting gaps, identifying risk, recognising and rewarding achievements
- •   assess future potential
- •   set performance objectives
- •   find out what motivates, and what rewards, the individual.

Appraisals should be:

- •   fair
- •   constructive

- objective
- positive
- unbiased
- open
- clear
- supportive
- developmental
- participative
- evidence-based
- problem solving
- collaborative
- challenging.

In recognition of this, it has been stipulated that GP appraisals will be:

- peer reviewed
- developmental
- not performance managed
- focused on process not clinical outcomes.

Appraisals may be defined as the process by which performance is reviewed periodically against the various requirements of the job. The personal development meeting, or appraisal, is primarily about the individual, their job and their development. The needs of the individual and the organisation they work within do not always coincide, so if conflict exists this should be explored. Those being appraised need to know what is expected of them, and to obtain fair, constructive, objective and positive feedback on how they are performing. Appraisals should be conducted within an environment that is open, positive, supportive and developmental.

The appraisee has the opportunity to :

- engage in the discussion
- reflect on their own performance
- state needs and expectations
- seek clarification
- set meaningful targets – subjective and objective.

The process

- **Meetings** may be structured or *ad hoc*.
- The **style** can be informally formal or formally informal.
- The **model** can be:
  - one way, rated by the appraiser only
  - a joint process, self-rated and fed back by the appraiser
  - 360 degree, where both appraisee and appraiser jointly appraise.

- The **system** may be complex, with multiple point self-assessment forms, peer reports, rating scales, or simple, with samples of notes and conversation. Sources of information can be from:
  - patients – practice surveys, plaudits
  - superiors – reports on good performance from the senior partner, consultant colleagues, etc.
  - peer group – other team members, staff.

The system needs to be regularly evaluated to ensure the process works effectively and efficiently. All judgements must be evidence-based and sourced: made on the basis of sound information.

Examples of performance may be made along the following lines.

Clinical performance

- Audits.
- Referrals.
- Prescribing data.
- Complaints and plaudits.

Attitudes and personal effectiveness

- Patient approach.
- Communication skills.
- Leadership skills.
- Contribution to the management process.
- Complaints and compliments.

Personal development

- Courses.
- Projects.
- Career plan.

Whatever system is adopted, goals must be set, and those goals must be:

- specific
- achievable
- measurable
- realistic
- time bound.

An example

What is to be achieved	How I will know when I have been successful	What I need to do	What help I need	Timescales
To take responsibility for the emergency surgery calls.	• Dealt with all emergency calls. • Made appropriate patient appointments.	• To learn about the internal telephone system. • To learn about the appointment system.	Training: • morning on telephone • computer training • talk with mentor about protocols.	• Training on telephone and appointments: week 1. • Aim to take duty responsibility alone by week 2.

The end result of the appraisal process is the individual's performance portfolio, which will sit alongside and feed into a Personal Development Plan, which will feed into the revalidation process, thus forming part of the clinical governance arrangements of the PCT:

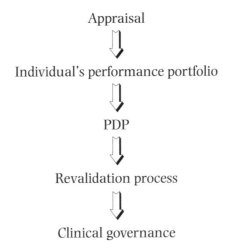

Appraisal

Individual's performance portfolio

PDP

Revalidation process

Clinical governance

⇨ **For the whole team**

Having read through this, what do you see as some of the disadvantages of appraisals?

Some possible answers

- What if the culture of the organisation is not open, but hierarchical?
- Surely the way the appraisal documents are constructed affects the outcome?
- It sounds time consuming but unless done regularly, it will not provide enough information.
- How can you avoid offending or upsetting people?
- How can we build in flexibility? Some jobs are easier to measure than others.
- It's just another form filling exercise.
- How can it not involve prejudice and subjectivity?
- What if we do not have the personal skills to develop this?[7–8]

How are you going to address these challenges?

Does your organisation:

- behave in an open way
- have a strong and gifted team
- reinforce mutual support
- learn from its mistakes
- believe in the importance of service delivery
- train and develop staff
- self-evaluate?

Appraisal processes will differ between organisations. Whatever style is chosen, check it meets the needs of all involved:

- the public
- the PCT
- your colleagues
- the individual clinician
- your organisation.

Introducing an appraisal system that meets everyone's needs should be a positive, strengthening experience, which should build on the strengths of both the organisation and the individuals working within it.

Practice PDPs

This is a public document, made available for scrutiny by the PCT. This document feeds into the local workforce planning document (the HImP) and should contain:

- GPs' PDPs

- practice nurse revalidation documents
- annual staff appraisals, including their own personal development or learning plans.

In this way, whole practice teams develop self-awareness, become more adept at critical and self-appraisal, and so become empowered and motivated to develop, learn and increase their job satisfaction.

Performance indicators

Health authorities and PCGs have developed these as an aid to assessing some care aspects in general practice. Clinical governance issues will now be added to their agenda. Is the practice aware of these checks, and are systems in place to prevent the risk of any complaints being upheld? Performance indicators include the following:

- numbers of formal complaints against GPs upheld
- unjustified patient removal requests
- failure to apply for PGEA
- prescribing indicators: high frequency benzodiazepines
- clinical indicators: adherence to CDM programmes
- standards of medical record summaries
- comparisons of IOS payments.

Informed consent

(*See* also Chapter 13)

⟹ **For the whole team**

What are the issues you need to consider around informed consent?

Some questions to ask yourself

○ Do you have a policy?

- ○ Are all patient groups covered?
- ○ Are you sure everyone understands the concept?
- ○ How do you make certain those with reading or learning difficulties understand what consent they are giving to research or treatments?

To cover yourselves, give as much information as possible. Give out patient leaflets or letters that:

- explain false negative and false positive results
- outline the limitations of screening.

The role of nurses and other NHS workers

'Let's get together and feel alright.'

Bob Marley

What do you expect the nurses' role to be in all this? What about other workers – social workers, therapists, counsellors, physiotherapists, occupational and speech and language therapists? How can their roles be developed so that they further complement and assist practitioners in delivering healthcare? What are the barriers to team working? There are professional barriers, often set up because of historic power imbalances, different training, different regulations. We all have difficulty sharing or relinquishing power. How will the new working regulations alter your professional relationships? If nurse triage is adopted to improve access, and a good skill mix across all the professionals is made use of, the GPs' workload will alter. Will this matter?

What about using more complementary therapies in primary care? A recent (2000) BBC poll showed that:

- 1 in 5 people want complementary medicine
- 48% want herbal medicine
- 21% want aromatherapy
- 6% want massage

to be available.[9]

What are your concerns about this?:

- ○ the cost
- ○ the fact treatments are private so the new services do not address inequalities
- ○ safety
- ○ training
- ○ regulations?

But these services do fit into the wider health agenda; they may be considered non-essential, but they are what the public want.

There is the opportunity now to review everyone's roles within general practice, the community and secondary care. Here we will concentrate on the nurses' role within general practice. That of the other core professions is a debate being taken up in PCGs and Community Trusts in particular.

Practices need to ensure that nursing time is well spent. The indication is that nurses should undertake more basic and advanced training to meet clinical governance requirements. The latest expectation is that nurses take over much of the routine GP work, so freeing up doctors to concentrate on the parts of medicine they best deliver.

What are the pros and cons of this? Are doctors going to miss seeing the 'worried well'? Are your nurses ready to take on a broader and more responsible role?

In order to develop the nursing role, practices will need to:

- think about what services could be safely devolved
- involve nurses
- inform nurses
- train nurses
- develop, write and review clinical protocols.

The same maxim applies here as it has elsewhere in the book: measure, analyse, instigate change and monitor.

Patient services

Have your nurses set up the following disease registers? Are they involved in chronic disease management of:

- asthma
- diabetes
- hypertension
- CHD or CVD
- smoking
- mental health?

Which of the following core (GMS) services do your nurses offer? Are they trained for this and updated regularly? Sixty six percent of MDU claims for practice nurse activity are as a result of perforating the ear drum during ear syringing. Don't make your practice a statistic.

What are your recording systems, and have you clear protocols in place for the following:

- telephone triage
- minor surgery assistance
- wound care
- counselling
- spirometry
- childhood vaccinations and immunisations
- adult vaccination and immunisations
- travel vaccinations
- hypertension monitoring
- ECG recordings
- venapuncture
- ear syringing
- contraceptive care
- menopause
- cervical cytology?

Many practices use highly qualified practice nurses to chaperone patients – is this really an appropriate use of their time and skill? Have you considered appointing healthcare assistants for this or encouraging relatives and friends to accompany patients if requested? (But not receptionists!) Have you costed this?

Training

Do you appraise your nurses, and do you keep written records of their competencies? Nurses now have a mechanism for demonstrating their professional competence, which is similar to the process undertaken by therapists, psychologists and the like.

Post-Registration Education and Practice (PREP) – UKCC (Nursing)

PREP is a continuing education programme for nurses and is an essential element of maintaining registration on the UKCC central register. It became mandatory under law in 1995. The standards are not dissimilar to the current Continuing Medical Education, and the new revalidation proposals. The core aim is to drive up nursing standards by developing individuals in four ways.

1   Notification of practice

To be completed:

- when a nurse applies to renew his/her registration three-yearly
- if the nurse changes his/her area of practice, e.g. from practice nurse to a nursing home
- if the nurse returns to work after a break of more than five years.

2   Professional development

- Each registered nurse must undertake a minimum of 35 hours of study every three years – this is separate from the RCN's continuous education points system.
- Nurses may select from a broad range of topics relevant to their present work:
  - care enhancement
  - practice development
  - risk reduction
  - educational development
  - patient, client and colleague support.

3   Personal professional profile

This is similar to that proposed for GPs: a confidential, reflective record of the nurse's career to date, recording learning experiences, which may be used as an information source for appraisals and to aid the assessment of current practice standards.
   This should be:

- confidential
- analytical
- evaluative
- reflective
- an aid to future planning
- able to demonstrate experiential learning
- appreciative of abilities, achievements and experience.[10]

There is a UKCC recommendation that all nurses in practice are supported or mentored by colleagues, and that time is allowed for reflection of practice.

○ Does this happen in your practice?
○ What is stopping it? Time? Geography? Lack of awareness?
○ Do your nurses have annual appraisals?
○ If so, who does them?
○ Have you got clear lines of accountability and responsibility for nurses?
○ Are nurses involved in practice and team meetings?
○ Do you keep a record of the training undertaken in your practice, when and by whom?
○ What percentage of training is formal and accredited and what is *ad hoc*?

4 *Other recommended training needs*

These include:

- nurse prescribing
- depression management
- substance misuse
- minor injuries and illness.

The following should be developed locally with multi-disciplinary team involvement:

- child protection
- resuscitation
- anaphylaxis.

⇒ **For the doctors and nurses**

Here are some questions to ask yourself about your nursing team.

Recommended levels of nursing care within a practice

The current nationally accepted (UKCP) levels of practice nursing care are 0.25 WTE per 1000 patients, or nine hours per week per 1000 patients.

○ How does your practice measure up?
○ When did your nurses join you?
○ Do you have any retirement or recruitment implications?
○ Do you have fewer than two nurses in your practice? If yes, there may be difficulties in releasing them for study, sick or maternity leave.

Skill mix

Practices often appoint their nurses without due thought for their skills or potential role within the practice. They then find they are committed to pay an inappropriate grade. When recruiting, think well about how to match skill to need: there is usually potential to use lower grades as healthcare assistants.

○   Do you automatically review your nursing needs each time you re-appoint?
○   Do your nurses have contracts based on Whitley terms and conditions?
○   Do all your nurses have clear and updated job descriptions?
○   What grades are your nurses?
○   Do you pay incrementally or based on responsibility or length of service?
○   Have you got a good range of skills and grades in your practice, or are all nurses grade G?
○   Are any of your nurses dual qualified, e.g. hold midwifery or district nurse qualifications?
○   Do they have any additional qualifications: ENB family planning, mentor skills, advanced diplomas in family planning, CHD or cervical cytology?
○   Do they visit patients at home? Why? What are you using your district nurses for?
○   How many hold a practice nurse qualification?
○   Have they got any qualifications that are not used?
○   Do you have any special skills in-house, e.g. a nurse practitioner or nurse prescriber?

Nurses should hold personal professional indemnity cover in their own right, not be covered by their employer MDU cover only.

Healthcare risks

See also the Health and Safety section in Chapter 7. Risk management during clinical procedures is primarily directed at patient outcome, but risks to clinical staff should also be considered. Think of the following procedures:

• sterilisation
• spillage
• infection
• needlestick injury
• dangerous substances
• clinical equipment
• medications
• clinical waste.

Your nurses are well placed to:

- assess the situation
- take action:
  - control
  - substitute
  - ensure safe packaging
  - transport
  - ensure safe handling arrangements are in place.

Clinical governance challenges for all clinicians

- Check all your GMC registrations are valid.
- Check your education status.
- Think now about ways to improve the quality of your clinical data.
- Think about how you are ensuring continuing professional development.
- Check eligibility for undertaking specific clinical procedures.
- Keep up to date with latest NSFs, clinical governance procedures, etc.
- Ensure you have high quality systems in place for clinical record keeping (medical records should be kept in good order) and collection of relevant information.
- Controls assurance: have a systematic self-assessment procedure in place to identify and manage clinical risk.
- Have clinical audit systems in place, and identify which areas are audited.
- Check you have a method of reporting adverse healthcare events.
- Ensure lessons are learned from this, so avoiding recurrence of similar events.
- Follow procedures.
- Communicate clearly.
- Treat each patient as an individual.
- Learn to be an effective team player.
- Respect your team.
- Encourage sharing of good practice.
- Assist others.
- Support the principle of standards.
- Voice your concerns.
- Develop quality – provide good clinical leadership.
- Develop evidence-based practices.
- Aim for outcomes.

Remember that poor clinical performance will be detected earlier and acted on quicker than ever before.

Writing model contracts for all clinical staff

Here are some suggested constituents of a contract for clinical, medical and non-medically qualified staff providing services in the NHS:[11]

Qualifications	Practitioners should be in receipt of a recognised qualification from a training establishment which is accredited by a suitable regulatory body.
Registration	Practitioners must be registered with a recognised professional body which requires its members to abide by codes of conduct, ethics and discipline.
Insurance	Practitioners must have adequate professional indemnity insurance cover that applies to the period of their employment.
Consent to treatment	Patients must be fully informed about the nature of the therapy and its effects, including any side effects, and have realistic expectations of its benefits. The informed consent of the patient or, in the case of young children, of the parent or guardian, must be gained and documented.
Medical responsibility	Practitioners should be aware that patients referred to them for treatment remain the overall responsibility of the referring clinician. Practitioners should not advise discontinuing existing orthodox treatments without the agreement of the referring clinician.
Documentation	A written record should be kept by practitioners of the consultation and each episode of treatment. All written (and oral) information should be treated as confidential and take account of the needs of the Data Protection Act and Caldicott review.
Refusal to treat	Practitioners have a duty not to treat a patient if they consider the treatment unsafe or unsuitable.
Education and training	Practitioners should take responsibility for keeping abreast of developments in the practice of their therapy.
Quality standards	Practitioners, in conjunction with other healthcare professionals, should assist with the development of local standards and guidelines for practice.
Audit	Practitioners should undertake clinical audit and should report results to the employing or commissioning practice/PCG. They should be responsible for monitoring the outcome of therapy; opinions of patients should be actively sought and included in any evaluation.
Research	Practitioners should be expected to agree to take part in research trials to support the evaluation and development of treatment programmes.
Health and safety	Practitioners should comply with the requirements of Health and Safety legislation and adhere to good practice in the protection of staff, patients and the public.
Control of infection	Practitioners should adhere to regulations governing infection control and follow the procedure for reporting outbreaks of infection.

Source: adapted from The Scottish Office/Department of Health (1996) *Complementary Medicine and the National Health Service.*

Make sure all your contracts for clinical staff within the practice comply with these standards.

Challenges for managers

There are major implications for individuals, organisations and the NHS in introducing clinical governance. The challenges for managers managing clinicians will be in:

- assisting and encouraging the development of leadership skills and knowledge amongst clinicians
- developing the appropriate accountability structures
- integrating continuing professional development into quality improvement programmes
- encouraging and developing more formal links between primary and secondary care
- implementation of evidence-based practice
- supporting and developing the IT clinical information infrastructure
- ensuring that changing practice occurs in the light of audit, research, complaints and risk management
- development of mechanisms to ensure that clinical audit is integrated into the organisation
- assisting and supporting the development of multi-disciplinary and inter-agency working.

⇒ **For the manager**

Some questions to ask yourself:

- What levers and sanctions do you need in place to make this work?
- Are the processes you have set up amenable to monitoring?
- What are your reporting arrangements?

Effective working partnerships will ensure effective implementation of clinical governance. Check the health of your relationships with these groups:

- other general practices
- your PCG/T
- your local Trusts
- your attached staff
- the general public
- your patients
- health and social care
- local education and research specialists.

You will know when you've arrived when:

- adverse events and complaints are detected and investigated, and the lessons learnt applied
- all clinical practice is evidence-based
- clinical audit is integrated into the organisation, and the quality of data is of a consistently high standard
- clinical risk reduction mechanisms are in place
- poor clinical performance is identified early, and dealt with quickly
- continuing professional development programmes are in place for all staff, clinical and administrative.

References

1   World Health Organisation (1989) The principles of quality assurance. *Quality Assurance in Healthcare.* **1**: 79–95.

2   Maxwell R (1981) Quality assessment in health. *BMJ.* **288**: 1470–2.

3   Department of Health (1996) *NHS Psychotherapy Services in England: review of strategic policy.* The Stationery Office, London.

4   Roth A and Fonagy P (1996) *What Works for Whom: a critical review of psychotherapy research.* Guilford Press, New York.

5   Ferguson E *et al.* (2000) A competency model for general practice: implications for selection, training and development. *Br J Gen Prac.*

6   British Association of Medical Managers (1999) *Appraisal in Action.* BAMM, Stockport.

7   Cole AG (1993) *Personnel Management* (3e).

8   Scheier, Geis and Wert (1987) Performance appraisals: no appointment needed. *Personnel J.* **November**: 80–7.

9   NHS Alliance (2000) *Complementary Medicine: information pack for primary care groups.* NHS Alliance, London.

10 Richardson A (1998) Personal professional profiles. *Nursing Standard.* **38**: 35–40.

11 NHS Alliance (2000) *Integrated Healthcare: a guide to good practice.* NHS Alliance, London.

Further reading

Lilley R with Lambden P (1999) *Making Sense of Risk Management: a workbook for primary care.* Radcliffe Medical Press, Oxford.

Moore R and Moore S (1995) *Health and Safety at Work: guidance for general practitioners.* Practice Organisation Series 1. RCGP Publications Unit, London.

Publications on evidence-based practice

Bandolier: a monthly newsletter describing healthcare effectiveness. Available from The Pain Relief Unit. The Churchill Hospital, Oxford OX3 7JL www.jr.ox.ac.uk/bandolier/index.html

Effective Healthcare Bulletins: NHS Centre for Reviews and Dissemination, University of York, York YO1 5DD; subscriptions from Royal Society of Medicine Press, PO Box 9002, London W1A 0ZA.

Health Updates: Health Education Authority, Trevelyan House, 30 Great Peter Street, London SW1P 2HW.

General Practice Risks: management and practice: www.croner.co.uk

Quality Assessment in General Practice: www.npcrdc.man.ac.uk

For leaflets and further information about clinical risk management and health and safety issues:

Scriptographic Publications Ltd
Channing House
Butts Road
Alton
Hants
GU34 1ND

Tel: 01420 541738

CHAPTER 6

Prescribing

Managing prescribing: reduce prescribing costs and improve clinical care

The following are some prescribing facts from 1998–9.

- Two-thirds of items prescribed were generic.
- The number of items dispensed rose by 3.2%.
- More than four-fifths of prescription items dispensed were free to patients.
- The average cost per prescription item increased 9%.
- The government introduced a maximum price scheme for generics.[1]

The government aims are for pharmacists and nurses to both prescribe and advise patients more, and in view of this they are developing patient group directives and encouraging prescribing incentive schemes. They aim to:

- make it easier for patients with chronic conditions to obtain repeat prescriptions
- by 2004 have NHS Direct referring people directly to their local pharmacy for help (trials in Scotland are already underway)
- make an even wider range of OTC medicines available.

Prescribing is now an element of the PCG/T budget, so you have the opportunity to:

- comment on prescribing practice and budgets, usually through your PCG
- use your budget to improve the cost and clinical care of your patients.

If you have not already done so, set up quarterly or six-monthly prescribing review meetings with your local pharmacist or PCG advisor. Here time can be set aside to look at and analyse your PPA reports and any additional information sent to you on indicative prescribing from your PCG/T, or join your local clinical governance/prescribing group run by your PCG/T, where you can keep informed through being part of the wider discussion.

At these meetings, you will be looking at prescribing issues such as:

- dosage
- cost
- efficacy
- palatability
- side effects
- patient compliance
- concordance
- convenience

through various noted high cost or high use drug groups.

You will then be part of a wider clinical discussion, during which your pharmaceutical colleagues will make various best practice recommendations, which may include:

- no change
- switching patients to better tolerated, cheaper or more effective drugs or dosages
- noting potential increases in drug spends, e.g. where best practice actually increases cost, such as the recommendation to medicate before investigation in gastroenterology
- noting where expenditure is decreasing because of additional clinics, e.g. if leg ulcer clinics are held, there is an increased staff cost but shift in the spend on dermatology and antibiotic prescribing
- devising a method for noting where colleagues who are high spenders can alert practice of any high cost patients, e.g. community nurses
- taking action to remove repeat prescribing and calling the patient in for consultation, e.g. for hypnotics and anxiolytics
- where to use brand names not generics and vice versa
- auditing which patient groups are receiving a particular drug, e.g. gluten-free products being inappropriately prescribed for drug users who use them to limit food bills
- noting the likelihood of dependency on some medications, and removing them from the computer so all scripts have to be handwritten
- noting where it is cheaper to prescribe the same drug but alter the dose or the amount prescribed to avoid wastage, e.g. prescribe 28- not 30-day packs of HRT medication
- noting where to remove 'as directed' from the computer and leave space for the doctor to write in free text
- where to opportunistically review, check or archive old medications
- when to alert the PCG/T or health authority if any exceptional high spends are expected, e.g. terminal cancers
- noting that blanket switch to generics is not a guarantee to contain prescribing costs.

Hints on managing prescribing costs

- Focus on controlling the volume of prescribing.
- Limit the uptake of new and expensive drugs.
- Control the costs of expensive modified release and combination products.
- Monitor hospital-initiated prescribing.
- Prescribe generically only where it will result in savings.

Prescribing indicators and targets

Most PCG/Ts are supporting practices wishing to reduce prescribing costs, and to further this have set up prescribing indicators using national recommendations. These will usually then be discussed further at PCG level, and decisions can then be made based on what would work locally. The indicators usually fall into specific drug groups.

For some questions for the practice to consider and an example of one practice's action to reduce their prescribing spend, *see* the website.

'The brown bag review' repeat prescribing project

Here is an example of how another practice set up a mechanism for reviewing and reducing their costs on repeat prescribing.

Some notes about the practice

- The practice already had their own formulary.
- They held quarterly prescribing meetings with the local health authority pharmaceutical advisor present.
- They had already identified a particular problem with their mental health spend through PPA reports.
- Part of the reason for the project was to try and identify and contain the costs of spending, with the additional gain of 'proving' to the health authority their valid attempts to keep within budget and their need for additional resources.
- The project began in late 1997, so the problems are topical to that period, but the same principles can be applied today.

The first stage of the project was to:

- overview and update computer system: input the formulary, set default instructions and quantities and update generic prescribing

- check and submit high cost items and claims and obtain equivalence of quantities.

Through this work, several problems were identified. These are summarised below with some management recommendations.

Costs

The practice noted an exponential increase in prescribing costs over the previous year, which were partly explained by the (then) new high cost antipsychotic drugs (olanzapine and risperidone in particular). The practice also noted increases in other areas, generated by applying new secondary care led protocols in order to limit referral costs and improve patient care, e.g. ulcer healing and lipid lowering drugs.

The practice undertook a mental health prevalence analysis which demonstrated their particular practice pressures, which they felt accounted for a higher than average CNS spend. The reported prevalence of psychotic disorders in practices in London and the South East was then 1.7 per thousand. A practice this size would expect 20. They had 140 patients registered (the practice had GMS responsibility for a local homeless project).

The other increases were hard to identify and explain. The practice noted their problems in identifying savings, particularly, they felt, because they had been following local good practice guidelines. They noted the following.

- They had an excellent local clinical reputation.
- They acted on encouragement to follow recommended good clinical practice guidelines. They thus prescribed to reach Health of the Nation targets in chronic disease management (asthma and diabetes) plus CHD (hyperlipodemia).
- They ran a sexual health (family planning) clinic and had a reputation for excellence in women's medicine so identified additional high spends in infertility, gynaecology and osteoporotic medication/HRT.

They referred to a current PACT analysis, which demonstrated they were still below health authority and national equivalents by 4% and 2% respectively, but the gap was narrowing considerably.

The practice felt that savings could be made with tighter clinical and managerial controls. A repeat prescribing model was presented.

Repeat scripts

It was noted that two-thirds of all GP prescriptions were repeats and they represented four-fifths of total prescribing costs.

Management controls

The practice used a project plan mechanism for identifying who was responsible for what by when.

What	Who
Compliance check: identify patients who over- or under-use medication hrough recalling patients for review six monthly or annually.	local pharmacist
Ensure all patients have a clear indication of when their medication should be reviewed: computer generated invite to make an appointment.	practice
Flagging up on the computer: bringing the review date to the attention of the prescriber.	practice
Invite patients to delete any medication they no longer require; responsible administrator can then delete the old and add the new.	practice
Clinical controls Authorisation: the decision that a repeat prescription is appropriate, the drug is effective and still needed, ongoing and at review.	GPs
Devise a mechanism for identifying how prescribing is initiated for: • patients with changes in drugs started by the hospital • newly registered patients.	practice manager
Recommend: • new medication changes go on the computer as soon as hospital letter received into practice • patients asked to bring in their hospital care plan or medication if recently discharged.	practice
Develop a standard review procedure for: • hypnotics • NSAIDs • anti-ulcer treatments.	GPs

Community pharmacist's role

Patient recall and check:

- dosage
- compliance
- poly-pharmacy
- form of medicine
- if any additional self-medication
- increased susceptibility, e.g. if older, any contraindications or caution required
- pharmaco-kinetics, e.g. tissue concentrations in the elderly as limited reserves of renal function[2]

- adverse reactions, e.g. in elderly, postural hypotension, confusion, ability to drive
- to communicate with patients to:
  - simplify regime
  - explain
  - instruct (health and safety)
  - clarify
- computer update:
  - placing directions on computer system and deleting 'as directed', especially for the elderly
  - culling historical repeat medication list so patients are less likely to obtain incorrect repeats.

Additional recommendations

- An audit of a sample of repeats to give an assessment of clinical controls.
- Liaison with practice staff to gain insight into what happens at present, introduce protocols giving more control, plan implementation and train.

Practice manager's role

To liaise with, and confirm administrative details with, the pharmacist and sponsors as follows.

- Apply to the local PCG/T or health authority for project funds and progress the project as soon as it is confirmed in writing.
- Manage the pharmacist: set out a tight agenda and work timetable and specify the outcomes.
- Confirm the day and time of attendance if the pharmacist is working with the practice computer on site – a networked terminal will need to be available. If time and space is limited, make this a defined and regular commitment.
- Agree payment for the pharmacist's time (currently around £25.00–£30.00 per hour).
- Make the final month's payment dependent on receipt of a written report clarifying the benefits (or not) of the scheme, as future funding will be dependent on a good outcome of the review.
- Liaise with the office manager to appoint patients for their 'brown bag review'.
- Give pharmacist a contract specifying (as per Data Protection Act 1998):
  - confidentiality
  - clear guidelines of accountability

With a copy to GPs to avoid likelihood of the pharmacists being swamped with additional (and unplanned) work while they are on site.
- Build in regular meetings to check you are on target.

Advantages

The advantages of this project were seen to be:

- better prescribing
- improved patient care
- enhanced clinical monitoring
- drug cost savings
- reduced risk of medical litigation
- decreased risk of accident through removing old medication from people's homes
- enhanced and improved hospital/community interface by improving the information base when GPs refer to secondary sector.

Obstacles

- Time – especially GP time.
- Resistance to change.
- Cost:
  - use notes to apply for additional project funds from your health authority or PCG/T
  - ask local pharmacist to work co-operatively as a smooth procedure will save their time
  - note the benefits to the pharmacist of joint working – it benefits them to develop an ongoing working relationship with their local GP practice, as this is where most of their repeat business occurs.

Specific outcomes anticipated

- Fewer scripts to be presented for signing.
- A reduction in poly-pharmacy.
- Scripts programmed with directions instead of 'as directed'.
- Reduced waste through correct dosage and limiting supply.

Write a practice formulary

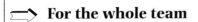 **For the doctors**

- If you use a formulary, what arrangements have you in place for accommodating emerging new drugs?
- Given that most GPs will prefer to prescribe according to the needs of individual patients, what do you feel would be a reasonable rate of compliance with a formulary?
- What triggers the review mechanism?
- Is your population stable or transient?
- How would this affect your budget?
- Do you have a practice based nurse prescriber?
- How can you measure their prescribing costs?
- Do you have any mutually beneficial joint business schemes with your local pharmacist, e.g. patient script delivery?

Reducing risk from prescribing

Do you have any prescribing policies in your practice?

All drugs have side effects, and some patients would become seriously ill if their medication were delayed. Measures need to be in place to reduce these risks to patients, and such administrative practices sharpen and improve clinical care and may even reduce the budget.

 For the whole team

Do you have a prescribing protocol to include:

- a system for GPs to learn about their prescribing patterns
- details about ready access to a pharmacist
- agreement for doctor-only signatures, countersignatures, additions or corrections
- thorough and regular updates and staff training for ancillary staff dealing with scripts
- signing of blank scripts forbidden
- details of any nurse prescribing
- frequency of updating records?

Do you have a repeat prescribing protocol to include:

○ a system to inform patients of access arrangements over extended holiday periods
○ a system to prevent fraud
○ secure storage of repeats
○ a system for checking who collects the scripts
○ a standard or time limit for collection
○ a system for recording repeat scripts in medical records
○ understanding that scripts will not be given more than a few days before their due date
○ only written, not oral, requests accepted
○ standards set out for the time between receipt and production
○ password identified access for staff who use the computer to generate repeat scripts?

An example application of a prescribing policy

An antibiotic prescribing policy

It is known that the majority of the population will take biotics at some time in their lives, and, apart from analgesics, no other drug is in such widespread use. Uniquely, the effectiveness of the antimicrobial agent in an individual patient can be affected by previous use in other individuals. There is no other area of prescribing in which the patient's expectations play such a role in determining whether to prescribe or not.[3]

The increasing emergence of antibiotic resistance has led to more effective use of antimicrobials becoming a national priority, with clinical governance as the overriding process within the NHS with which to drive the changes locally.

For primary care the current principles are:

• no prescribing of antibiotics for simple coughs and colds or viral sore throats
• to limit prescribing for uncomplicated cystitis for three days in otherwise fit women
• to limit over-the-telephone prescribing to exceptional cases.

The following principles refer to antibiotic prescribing but can be applied across all prescribing in the practice. Use the questions to inform your prescribing policy, and refer to having such a policy in the business plan. This would be a good pre-requisite for inclusion in a PMS or PMS+ application.

Issues within the practice

o   Who within the practice prescribes what and why?
o   What are the problems associated with antibiotics' inappropriate use?
o   How can change be effected within the practice?
o   Does everyone (doctors, nurse and receptionist) have a consistent line on antibiotic prescribing for self-limiting illness?
o   Are antibiotic scripts available over the phone?
o   Can patients get these scripts without being seen?
o   If the practice has reduced its antibiotic prescribing, does it then prescribe more of the very new, expensive ones to compensate?
o   Are educational leaflets and posters on reducing antibiotic use readily available throughout the practice, especially in consulting and treatment rooms?

Issues outside the practice

o   Are antibiotics freely available from co-operatives and deputising services or walk-in centres?
o   Does NHS Direct aim to reduce antibiotic expectations in your area?
o   What line do local pharmacies take?
o   What would be the likely reaction from the local media if there were a clamp down in antibiotic prescribing in your area?

Patient group directives

These documents are written to enable certain non-medical professional groups (e.g. nurses and pharmacists) to prescribe certain medicines to particular, and identified, patient groups. They are used where the presence in the population of particular illnesses or conditions significantly increase the workload of GPs, e.g.:

•   a flu epidemic where requests for zanamivir (Relenza) are increased
•   demand for emergency contraception
•   demand for anti-smoking medication (Zyban).

The government's intention is to assist GPs with workload reduction, and also to enable allied professionals to take on some of the clinical responsibilities for patients.

For the doctors

What do you see as the advantages and disadvantages of this approach?

Some advantages

- Prescribing to assist patients entitled to free scripts (useful where the cost of a drug previously allowed over the counter (OTC) has significantly increased to put it out of reach of the population requiring it).
- Supporting local initiatives, e.g. stopping smoking or using emergency contraception to reduce local unwanted teenage pregnancy rates.

Issues to consider for patient group directives

- When will the directive be actioned?
- Under what circumstances will it be actioned, e.g. once the required critical mass of disease in the population is reached?
- Who will the directive be applied to – pharmacists or nurses?
- Under what criteria?
- Formulated within whose guidance – NICE? local guidance?
- Will there be any need to apply additional local guidelines to reduce prescribing risks in your population?
- Who will require training?
- When will this training occur?
- Who will inform the responsible GPs when the drug has been prescribed?
- Under what circumstances will the GP be informed, e.g. will the GP be informed by fax if a pharmacist has either seen and/or recommended Relenza to any patient seen face to face, or been contacted by phone by a patient who lives within the patch?
- Who needs to be consulted on the directive, and who needs to sign off the recommendations – the LMC, the PCT or the health authority?
- Who needs to have copies of the directive?
- What feedback on progress is to be given, when and to whom?

For the doctors

What do you see as the advantages of using pharmacists, not practice nurse triage, when using patient group directives?

Some possible reasons

- Pharmacists could buy in and supply the medication easily.
- Work would be diverted away from practices.
- Practice nurses have easier access to a GP.

Some more considerations

- Does your PCG/T have a prescribing forum?
- How can you be involved?
- Does it produce a prescribing newsletter?
- Does your local microbiology department send out regular information?
- If not, would you be prepared to organise this?

Prescribing strategies – a carrot or stick approach?

GPs will be aware that their PCG/T has a prescribing strategy, which has usually been discussed and agreed locally with individual or representative GPs. The main issue for GPs is usually target setting: the main hinge for this is the prescribing incentive scheme. However, the methods used to encourage GPs to comply with local regulations and directives do not always work.

What do you consider to be the best ways of managing change within practices to achieve the desired outcome? Mark if you agree or disagree with the following, and note what you see as the advantages and disadvantages of each approach.

---

1 **Target high spending practices by visiting pharmacy advisors, who have access to, and can analyse, local PACT data.**

Problem:

- intimidating
- expensive
- no change effected.

---

2 **Encourage practices to develop a relationship with their community pharmacists who can assist with analysis of practice prescribing patterns.**

Problem:

- training and control issues as independent relationships set up between pharmacists and GPs
- local pharmacists do not have access to PACT data
- many urban GPs use multiple local pharmacists.

---

3 **Use trained facilitators to assist practices with PACT analysis and manage the change – identifying the problems, goal setting and managing the processes required.**

Problem:

- local facilitators not always pharmaceutically trained.

---

4 **Implement managed care solutions, where pharmacists link with practices to change select drug groups.**

Problem:

- ownership
- continued change.

---

5   Encourage GPs to use a computer system such as PRODIGY, which analyses individual and collective prescribing patterns and encourages a formulary approach.

Problem:

- many GPs cannot be persuaded to use their computers at every consultation.

---

6   Naming and shaming: Give practices access to practice-identifiable information on local and individual prescribing rates and costs, demonstrating their position in the local league tables. This can stimulate the debate, reinforce the idea of a communal budget and help effect change.

Problem:

- fear of identity and intimidation, potentially humiliating rather than constructive.

Finally – read your PACT data

GPs need to consider:

- where they fit in relation to the rest of the locality, in both cost and volume of prescribing: sometimes unexpected and regressed change occurs, e.g. a tendency for GPs to prescribe high cost antibiotics whilst reducing the overall volume
- setting sensible targets to achieve change
- the use of drugs licensed for one condition being used to treat another condition for which the drug is not licensed
- areas where patient education can achieve change
- remaining open and questioning the validity of local or national guidance
- consideration of compliance, cost, concordance, and convenience
- the evidence base and safety of drugs in particular age groups
- efficacy: where there is a tendency to use sub-therapeutic doses, the need to titrate up lower doses until effective
- which drugs they have control over and which are initiated by secondary care colleagues
- how these secondary care costs can be contained, through patient education or GP/secondary care education links
- where variations can be explained by repeat prescribing cycles
- which drug companies are willing to sponsor product change.

Managers need to consider all of the above, plus:

- the difficulty of operating a number of such initiatives with reduced resources.

References

1   Department of Health (2000) *DoH Statistical Bulletin. Prescriptions Dispensed in the Community: England 1998–99.* DoH, London.

2   *British National Formulary* No. 34 (September, 1997). BMA and RPSGB, London.

3   National Prescribing Centre and Edgecumbe Health Ltd (2000) *Putting Clinical Governance into Practice. Managing antibiotic resistance: a practical guide.* NPC, Liverpool and Edgecumbe Health Ltd, Clifton.

Further reading

Prescribing Support Unit (1998) *Prescribing Measures and the Application: an explanation.* PSU, Leeds.

Roland M, Holden J and Campbell S (1999) *Quality Assessment for General Practice: supporting clinical governance in primary care groups.* National Primary Care Research and Development Centre, Manchester.

Zermansky A (1996) Who controls repeats? *Br J Gen Prac.* **46**: 643–7.

Further information

National Prescribing Centre
The Infirmary
70 Pembroke Place
Liverpool
L69 2GF

Tel: 0151 794 8137

www.npc.co.uk

CHAPTER 7

Communication within the practice

'Re-building public trust in doctors must emphasise that patients have the right to be critical.'

Donna Covey[1]

'Customer expectations about quality and value for money are increasing.'

Raj Vasudevan[1]

Some of the factors most commonly affecting clinical negligence claims are:

- communication breakdown
- poor systems and processes
- human error.[2]

Practices need to develop systems to manage clinical and administrative communications, e.g. home visit and telephone protocols, tracer systems for medical records and complaints procedures. Processes need to be put in place to integrate quality into all organisational processes. Quality is becoming everyone's business, and is an issue that can no longer be avoided.

The basic considerations to avoid communication breakdown across people or systems are to communicate, communicate, communicate!

- Plan ahead.
- Communicate (keep people involved and informed).
- Review and monitor systems and procedures regularly.
- Solve the problem – don't procrastinate.

I recommend practices use Lilley and Lambden's risk management ideas[3] as a guide to reducing these risks.

Considerations for doctors

 Practices often devise fair and equitable systems and guidelines, but then allow individuals to bend the rules.

- Encourage and reward systems to identify and acknowledge mistakes.
- Share good practice openly with your colleagues.
- Hold regular clinical team meetings.
- Listen to patients and evaluate their experiences.
- Implement and adhere to formal systems.
- Have procedures in place for monitoring new practitioners.
- Develop incident reporting methods.
- Have a system to review or audit medical records and prescribing management.
- Have a system for reviewing training needs and knowledge bases.
- Have patient consent procedures in place.
- Review patient access in case you inadvertently discriminate against any patients.
- Monitor unplanned re-admission and unexpected patient death procedures.
- Educate and feedback to staff.
- Date and sign all record entries.
- Establish a research and development culture.
- Ask yourself if your surgery absences are planned or *ad hoc*. Have you ever not arranged cover?
- If you devise a system, e.g. a partnership holiday rota, so not to be as reliant on locum cover for sickness and holidays, use it!

Risk manage your visiting doctors

Write a locum fact pack so all non-principals working in your surgery are familiar with daily and routine practice and referral procedures.

- Do you encourage visiting doctors to evaluate their practice?
- What is your mechanism for recording any adverse incidents? Devise a stamp for locums to use in medical records: 'Please report back any adverse or unusual events from this consultation/referral/treatment.'
- Could you devise a monitoring and reviewing mechanism so locums can receive feedback on their performance?
- Have you any retired friends who still locum for you? What is your criteria for selection? How is their experience and knowledge verified?
- How is the patient's view of locums or out of hours service taken into account?
- How do you measure performance?

○ Have you a mechanism for noting and recording inadequate practice?
○ How do you evaluate performance: do you measure registrar and locum prescribing and referral trends?
○ Who monitors the out of hours use and costs?

Administrative considerations

Re-visit your protocols for:

* visits, to ensure domestic visits/home visits are not late or missed
* urgent versus routine appointments
* missed or cancelled appointments
* telephone messages/advice/call-back procedures
* labelling, sending and receiving samples
* confirming messages are received and/or acted on
* confidentiality
* notifying patients of delays
* notifying patients of results
* checking outstanding referrals
* the practice post system
* returning patient records
* maintaining and repairing medical equipment.

How do you communicate within your practice? Make a list for the business plan. Do you:

○ circulate special newsletters
○ have weekly surgery bulletins
○ have away days
○ have regular meetings
○ network computers with bulletin boards and an e-mail facility?

The telephone is often the first point of call into general practice so it is essential to get the manner in which the phone is answered right. Whether a consultation call or appointment request, make certain these points are covered, if adapted:

* identify self and name of business
* gather essential data – especially address and telephone number
* establish what the caller wants and why
* give administrative information if required
* examine the caller, verbally
* explore the options together
* make decision
* document.

For nurses

- Ensure protocols are in place for all delegated clinical procedures.
- Check registration status and training needs.

Rule number 1: To limit losses and avoid breakdowns in communication, make explicit your expected standards, train the staff, and distribute requirements with all staff contracts.

For an example of expected standards for reception staff, *see* the website.

Rule number 2: Make sure all people working within the practice – for however long – receive an adequate induction to the job. This includes doctors.

For an example induction for GP registrars, *see* the website.

GP registrars need a gentle introduction to general practice. Their working experience to date will have taken place in a hospital environment: a larger institution with a more formal climate. Hospitals are run on strict hierarchical terms, with well defined protocols and clear ways of working, whereas general practices are very much more individualistic, determined by the personalities of the doctors and staff.

GP registrars will normally require a fuller induction than non-clinical staff. Ideally there should be at least a week's overlap with the last year's registrar to allow time for this – although expensive, a thorough induction will save time in mistakes and questioning later on.

So that the practice may get the best out of their registrar, and they themselves benefit from increased job satisfaction, a planned induction should include giving general and detailed information on the practice.

Additional questions for the practice

- Have you written a letter confirming appointment?
- Do you offer regular appraisals with a trainer?
- Has the registrar got a PDP?
- How frequently do they meet with the practice manager to check that all is well and that training needs are being met?

Rule number 3: Keep good records

○ Are your medical records accurate and reliable?
○ Are the notes summarised?
○ Is key data easily accessible and kept separate, e.g. prescribing?
○ Are records stored securely and are they easily accessible?
○ Are all contacts noted, including telephone contacts, secure and accessible?
○ Is filing up to date?
○ Are records kept of investigations sent off, acted on, and received?
○ What is the system for recording recent deaths, terminal illnesses, discharges from hospital – is this accessible to all?

Blowing the whistle

○ What happens if someone in the practice has serious concerns about clinical malpractice, fraud or theft? Has the practice got a procedure for raising these concerns?
○ Is everyone in the practice aware of it?
○ If you have not got such a procedure, do you know if your PCG/T has one?

The Public Interest Disclosure Act 1998 aims to promote accountability and openness within organisations. It gives a framework that enables anyone who has suspicions that a serious malpractice is taking place to report their concerns in a considered and responsible way. If anyone within the practice is concerned about what is happening at work, and the concerns are not easily resolved, it can be difficult for staff to know where to turn.

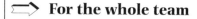 **For the whole team**

Make a note of some of the risks that you feel general practice faces. What could be seen as dangers to the practice, the public or the environment?

Some possible issues

- Poor clinical practice.
- Poor management practice.
- Treatment by unqualified personnel.
- Misuse of public funds.
- Serious errors.
- Failure to maintain proper records.
- Staff or doctor alcohol or substance addiction.
- Health and safety breaches.
- Breaches of confidentiality.
- Accidental or suspicious death or serious injury to anyone on premises.
- Abuse of patients, colleagues, staff or others (physical, sexual or psychological, e.g. bullying).

It is very probable that in the course of your working life someone within the practice will come across incidents or situations that give you cause for concern. If so, you and your staff should know the procedure to report it. Staff within the practice are going to be worried about raising such issues. It is particularly difficult for anyone within a small organisation to raise concerns. Any policy written should reflect the dynamics of the employer/employee relationship. Anyone should feel able to address legitimate concerns without fear of censure, or fear of appearing disloyal. Procedures should enable anyone in the practice to raise their concerns at an early stage and in the right way.

Who would be covered by such a policy?

- Agency staff and staff under contract for services.
- General practitioners, who, for the purposes of the above Act are deemed to be employed by the health authority.

When to raise concern

Questions to ask yourself

- Do all staff know when to use a whistle-blowing procedure?
- Do they know which procedure to use for other personal issues, e.g. a grievance procedure?
- Do they know what to do if an incident in the practice occurs which attracts the attention of the media? If approached for information by a journalist, it is wise for them politely to refuse to comment, and inform

whoever is responsible for communications at the PCG/T or health authority.
○ How are staff protected from victimisation?

One way to protect your staff is to make clear you are committed to such a policy. If staff raise a genuine concern, have an honest and reasonable suspicion that malpractice has happened, and are not acting for personal gain, they must be made aware they:

- will not be at risk of losing their job
- will not suffer any form of retribution
- will not suffer any harassment
- will have their identity protected where reasonably possible
- will be told about any action taken, provided this does not infringe any duties of confidence
- will be asked certain questions such as:
  - how they think the matter might best be resolved
  - if they have any personal interest in the matter
  - if their concern falls more properly within the grievance process.

Provided they act in good faith, it does not matter if they are mistaken. However, staff must be made aware that any malicious allegations could lead to disciplinary action being taken against them.

Whistle-blowing policies also need to stipulate how the practice will deal with any concerns raised. The following acts as an example.

Once you have told us of your concern, our action may involve an internal inquiry or a more formal investigation. We will also:

- *tell you who is handling the matter*
- *tell you how you can contact him/her*
- *tell you whether your further assistance may be needed*
- *tell you how we propose to handle it.*

Does your policy make clear:
○ to whom within the practice suspicions can be reported
○ when it may be advisable to contact an organisation outside the practice, e.g. an MP, the police or the media
○ who within the PCT or health authority will give advice on whom to contact, and in which circumstances
○ when to report concerns to a professional regulatory body, e.g. GMC, UKCC, etc.
○ who to go to if you remain unhappy with the response (usually the external auditor or your NHS Executive Regional Office)?

Where to go for further information

If you want free, confidential and legal advice about how to raise a concern about serious malpractice at work, contact:

- your own trade union (or contact the Certification Officer for Trade Unions and Employers' Associations) Tel: 020 7210 3734
- the independent charity Public Concern at Work Tel: 020 7404 6609
- Audit Commission Tel: 020 7828 1212
- Financial Services Authority Tel: 020 7676 1000
- Health and Safety Executive Tel: 020 7717 6000
- National Audit Office Tel: 020 7798 7000
- Serious Fraud Office Tel: 020 7239 7272
- The NHS fraud reporting number is: 08702 400100.

Confidentiality

(*See* also the section on the Data Protection Act on page 188)

 For the whole team

Do you have a confidentiality agreement?

The fundamental principle here is that healthcare workers must not disclose or use any confidential information obtained in the course of their work other than for the clinical care of the patient to whom that information relates.

What are the exceptions to this?

Some considerations

There are legal and medical exceptions which allow disclosure in exceptional circumstances, for example:

- patient consent to disclosure

- disclosure in the patient's own interest
- verbal and written reporting to the team
- disclosure required by law
- any overriding duty to society because of national security or public health concerns
- teaching and research
- the storage and transmission of records and information.

If in any doubt, consult with your professional body.

Communication with patients

'We are employed by the customer, they deserve more than our contempt.'

Notice in garage. For *'customer'* read *'patient'*

'The cultural flaws in the medical profession show up an excessive paternalism, lack of respect for patients and their right to make decisions about their care, secrecy and complacency about poor practice.'

Sir Donald Irvine, president of the GMC, January 2001

Practices can no longer afford not to involve patients in their decision making. To do so would perpetrate the kind of arrogant, paternalistic and hierarchical way of working that does not have a place in the modern health service – an attitude that reflects the tiredness, stress and prejudice of its workers.

Communicating well with patients takes time and energy, but done well it reduces risk. Here we look at some of the best ways to engage patients in participating in, and keep patients informed about, your practice. Those reading your business plan will be looking at the ways you keep in touch with your patients. Are you proactive or do you respond when the demand is made of you? Do you measure the level of complaints in the practice, and note the reason?

 General practice needs to overcome a reluctance in involving patients in service developments or even in their own treatments.

The new NHS requires that practices seek to identify and meet the health needs of the population they serve and embrace new technology to serve this end. Not all practices are committed to this. It is important to look at ways of helping patients to take responsibility for their own health through patient education. People who take an active interest in developing healthcare develop a broader understanding of health and disease. They begin to understand that health is affected by:

- social and economic factors: poverty, unemployment and social exclusion
- environmental factors: air and water quality, housing, food and safety
- lifestyle choices: diet, physical activity, use of drink and drugs and sexual behaviour
- access to good quality services: education, social care, health, local transport and leisure
- fixed factors, age, sex and genes.

Through being involved in discussions about healthcare provision, the hope is that they begin to develop responsibility for their health, and become less dependent on healthcare providers to meet their needs. Their involvement is particularly useful and welcome when making difficult or unpalatable rationing decisions.

 Practices must demonstrate an understanding of the concept of user involvement in the NHS.

Most practices need to further develop ways of working in partnership with patients. Where practices have already demonstrated their interest in developing their patient's voice, they could now consider:

- patient participation groups
- informal feedback systems, e.g. suggestion boxes
- health panels
- open meetings
- discussion/focus groups
- rapid appraisal (gathering information from key local informants)
- disease support groups
- interviews
- opinion polls
- neighbourhood forums
- practice based annual surveys
- appraisal systems such as customer panels
- postal questionnaires.[4]

⇒ **For the whole team**

What do you feel about involving the public? Note some of the pluses and minuses.

What do you consider the public wants from their health service?

Compare this with what national surveys show they want:[5]

- more and better paid staff
- reduced waiting times
- quicker access
- fewer cancellations
- new ways of working
- care centred on the patient not the system

- higher quality of care
- better facilities
- better conditions for staff
- better local services
- ending the postcode lottery
- more prevention.

How did your ideas match up?

Patients, especially those with chronic ill-health, know their experience of illness better than anyone else. Whatever their problem, it is theirs not ours. If patients feel empowered, they develop more choice. They are more likely to take control of their own illnesses, they learn and so become better informed and less passive. Once they are passive they become over-dependent on health professionals for their care, and become frequent attenders. If they are encouraged to be proactive, they enrich their lives and feel, and behave, less like victims. They take the lead.

Pause for thought

'Somewhere on the south coast of England there was an elderly care long stay hospital. One day the staff on one ward decided to ask patients what they wanted. What would improve the quality of their lives? There were three main things. Firstly, they did not have their own underwear: they all went into a sort of communal melting pot. Also they weren't given any choice over the way their hair was cut. A person would turn up on a certain day, and would cut their hair all the same way. A third source of irritation was that they had no say in what they were called. Some wanted to be referred to and spoken to as Mrs Smith, for instance, others wanted to be known by their first name.'

S Morris et al.[6]

Some ideas to consider

o   As a practice, do you listen to and involve your patients? How?
o   What action could you take to improve the knowledge, skills and attitudes of carers?
o   Do you see your patients as having the ability to solve problems, not just create them?
o   Do you know the difference between owning and controlling a situation and enabling it?
o   Do you feel that the public have a right to be involved (they are paying for the service), or that it is better left to the experts?
o   Are you really prepared for the effort, energy and cost needed to build the right relationship?
o   At what level do you see your responsibility for public health kicking in:
 –   patient level?
 –   practice level?
 –   community level?
 –   national level?
 –   international level?
o   Who do you consider as key in the process:
 –   social care?
 –   the voluntary sector?
 –   housing?
 –   transport?
 –   education?
 –   local shops and businesses?
o   What is most important for each of you:
 –   the idea?
 –   the process?
 –   the outcome?

- ○ Who has the skills needed for this work, namely:
  - – networking?
  - – listening?
  - – developing trust?
  - – understanding?

Patient surveys

Before you embark on constructing your own survey, find out if your PCG/T advocates using an established and valid one that already exists, such as the General Practice Assessment Survey. *See* the website.

See the website for an example of one practice's project to involve patients in service planning.

 For the manager and doctors

You may be asked to facilitate a patient group. Check you have experience of facilitating groups. Do you need more:

- ○ experience
- ○ understanding
- ○ knowledge
- ○ organisational skills
- ○ enthusiasm
- ○ time
- ○ energy
- ○ commitment
- ○ understanding of group dynamics
- ○ interpersonal skills
- ○ chairing skills
- ○ team building skills
- ○ experience of managing conflict
- ○ counselling skills?

Have you got up to date knowledge of secondary care and are you aware of some of the resource implications and service changes? Changes which could have major resource implications for health commissioners could include:

- more primary prevention with better drugs
- predictive genetic testing
- more widespread annual screening
- changes in the indications for treatment, earlier

- more expensive, more effective treatments
- more multi-professional care
- more home care
- a tendency to move care to larger units
- a tendency to increase training for all specialists
- for all patients, better:
    - symptom control
    - information on appropriate services
    - referral on
    - out of hours care
- development of clinical protocols with known efficacy.

How will these changes impact on you in primary care?

Patient literature

Once time is invested in writing this kind of information, practices reap the benefits as it is cheap and easy to update. Funds or sponsorship may be available from the PCG/T or a pharmaceutical company to support this kind of project. It improves communication, assists in managing risk, and supports clinical governance guidelines. The information provided here can be used as an appendix to the business plan.

Some pointers

- Ask each staff group to write their own copy.
- Edit it into your preferred house style.
- Give updated information about any new initiative, e.g. local Sure Start programmes run by health visitors.
- Remember to use appropriate language for your population: the average reading age in this country is around 11 years old – the level of a tabloid.
- Use plain English.
- Translate if required, and offer the document in Braille or audiotape.
- Use one word for two where possible.
- Keep all sentences short.
- Keep language personal: '*you*' instead of '*they*'.
- Avoid polysyllabic words.
- Avoid double negatives.
- Avoid jargon.
- The aim is to inform not impress.
- Repeat key information (telephone numbers etc.) several times.
- Use a large font and print black on yellow to make it accessible to those with visual impairments.

The New NHS Plan is asking that practices produce a wider range of information in their leaflets. Plan how you could inform your patients about:

- your list size
- accessibility
- performance against NSF standards
- number of patients removed.

Dealing with complaints

 For the practice manager

Consider the following statements. Which do you think best applies to your practice?

A   Copies of local information and contacts are kept in a file on display in the waiting area.
B   Copies of local information are kept in a file, and given out if requested.
C   We have some leaflets around somewhere.

A   We provide excellent and updated newspapers and magazines and have a children's play area.
B   We ask patients to bring in unwanted magazines for the reception area.
C   We find it difficult to keep all this literature up to date.

A   There is a complaints and plaudits book with a poster describing the procedures posted in the waiting area.
B   Everyone in the practice is aware of the complaints and plaudits procedure.
C   The manager knows about the complaints procedure.

A   Patients are given written and updated information about the repeat prescription service and appointments, and there is a noted system for informing patients about delays.
B   The practice is looking into better ways of alerting patients about delays when they can afford it.
C   Patients know and want too much already.

A   Patient records are available 90% of the time when the patient consults and this target is audited and updated regularly. At the last audit a tracer system was incorporated into the practice.

B   Patient records are not always available when the patient consults and this causes unnecessary delay and irritation throughout the practice. A receptionist has been disciplined.
C   There is no time for audit, we are too busy practising medicine.

A   The practice audits the complaints and plaudits, catagorises the reason for the failure, is open about naming the person responsible, collectively discusses ways to solve the problem and implements them.
B   We measure complaints, and always write and apologise to the complainer with a copy for the complaints file.
C   A named doctor deals with all the complaints in the practice.

A   We give patients copies of correspondence relating to them, with a glossary of medical abbreviations and terms.
B   GPs and nurses in the practice take time to explain the contents of letters if requested.
C   If the patient misinterprets information, the doctor asks them to make an appointment with the nurse, who can explain things to the patients better than a doctor can.

Every healthcare experience is personal, and is usually a mixture of excellent medical care and unacceptable incompetence or irritations.
    Common negative health experiences include the following:

* poor communication with patient
* poor communication with other professionals
* poor communication within the system
* variations in provision
* poor information
* lack of medical understanding/acknowledgement of the real, emotional issues affecting the patient and carers
* bureaucracy and hierarchies benefiting the system not patients.

We also need to be aware of the good stuff happening that helps primary and secondary care make the patient experience a better one:

* NSFs in cancer care, diabetes, CHD and elderly care
* NICE recommendations
* local centres of excellence
* collaborative care planning
* patient forums
* primary/secondary care protocols
* NHS Act 1999: more screening/assistance for carers/CHI/IT support
* individual and local initiatives, e.g. taped consultations in cancer care.

However, many of our patients do experience problems within the system, and complain. When this happens, the practice manager's role is not to ignore anecdotal evidence, but to pull together the evidence and present it back to his or her team so it can inform better practice in the future.

According to a recent report from the GMC the most common complaints needing resolution from general practice are:[7]

- care management – 35%
- associated with grief – 20%
- delayed or failed diagnosis – 12.7%.

 For the whole team

What are your solutions?

- Personal advice and an apology given over the telephone results in a higher level of complaints being resolved than apology by letter.
- Put the problem right immediately – do not cause the patient further delay or anguish.
- Your response must be real and important to you, otherwise it will be perceived as a standard, and impersonal, business response:
  - apologise first
  - acknowledge the patient's anxiety
  - acknowledge and understand the problem you have caused them
  - then give an explanation, but only if it is essential
  - finish with how you are going to put it right
  - thank the complainer for drawing your attention to the matter.

Sample letter

Thank you for writing and drawing our attention to ....

We are sorry that this caused you such upset, and concerned to hear that you were so inconvenienced by our mistake.

It has been our practice to ...., but it may well be we have to look at this again, as the system seems to be failing. We will certainly take the issue to our next practice meeting, where we discuss such incidents and try and find a way of resolving them./After discussion with all concerned, we have decided to ....

Thank you again for writing; we do appreciate it, as it is only through hearing of such mistakes that we can learn how to put things right for the future. If we can help any further please do contact X, who will do her best to assist.

Yours sincerely,

It is well documented that feelings such as fear, anxiety and loss of control greatly heighten physical and emotional pain and difficulties. It is therefore not surprising that those recently bereaved are more likely to both attend the doctor for their own recent onset of illness and also more likely to complain following the bereavement of a loved one.

Health and safety

The first step to making your workplace healthy and safe is to identify the risks. Then take steps to prevent accidents and ensure the good health of your employees.

Every employer has a duty to assess risks in the workplace, and all employers must follow a specific risk assessment plan. The first Health and Safety at Work Act (HASAWA) in 1974 created a broad base of duties which, if neglected, may allow an employer to be criminally prosecuted. Subsequent EEC directives have been issued which make employers' requirements more explicit.

A Health and Safety Risk Assessment provides a structured method aimed at protecting people, leading to effective action to control the major causes of harm. Employers need to:

- identify the hazards
- establish which are the most risky
- assess whether existing precautions are adequate
- devise plans to meet any shortcomings
- establish how changes can be introduced
- check that precautions are working
- control any risks or reduce them to insignificant levels
- record the assessment (if they have five or more employees).

The most common risks to general practice relate to:

- people
- procedures
- the working environment.

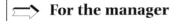 **For the manager**

Steps to risk assessment

- Look for the hazards.
- Decide who might be harmed and how. Patients? Children? Builders? Medical staff? Cleaners?

- Evaluate the risks arising from the hazards. Can you remove or contain the hazard without much cost to the practice? Can you minimise the hazard through training?
- Record the findings using the above points as a framework.
- Assess the effectiveness of precautions. If injuries occur or there are changes in patterns of work, incidents need to be investigated.
- Implementation:
  - aim to scrutinise and improve, not just to maintain and justify
  - deliver practical proposals
  - make a timetable for action
  - identify funds and who is responsible
  - communicate the changes.
- Audit and review:
  - was your action effective?
  - has the right overall decision been made?

Legal essentials

Do you:

- own a written safety policy?
- have a health and safety law poster or leaflet visible?
- consult with employees?
- have Employers' Liability Insurance?
- record and notify accidents?
- have clear first aid arrangements?

People and risk

Practices also need to consider protecting staff from:

- the effects of stress (workload, people, colleagues)
- violence
- ill-health
- damage from poor manual and handling procedures.

Healthcare risks

Risk management during clinical procedures is primarily directed at patient outcome, but risks to clinical staff should also be considered. Your nurses are well placed to:

- assess the situation
  - sterilisation

- spillage
- infection
- needlestick injury
- dangerous substances
- clinical equipment
- medications
- clinical waste
- take action
  - control
  - substitute
  - ensure safe packaging, transport and handling arrangements are in place.

The working environment

Look at the following risks. Who assesses and monitors these risks? Have you a policy in place that you regularly update?

- Fire
- Electricity
- Asbestos
- Atmosphere
- Heat
- Pollutants
- Lighting
- Flooring
- Movement flows
- Workstations
- Housekeeping
- Catering and food hygiene
- Cleaning
- Building maintenance
- Building works
- Space
- Noise
- Tidiness
- Equipment
- Manual handling/lifting
- Hazardous substances
- VDUs
- Waste disposal.

Checklist for your practice. Does your practice:

○ carry out a systematic assessment of workplace risks?

- record any significant findings (if you have five or more employees)?
- have a health and safety policy that covers protective and preventive measures?
- have a clear picture of who is responsible for which procedure?[8]

Try www.hawnhs.hda–online.org.uk for further information.

Improving security and preventing violence

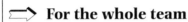 **For the whole team**

Make a list of all the incidents that have occurred in your surgery over the years that have challenged the security systems you have in place. Include any threatening behaviour from patients.

Here are some examples from other surgeries.

- Receptionist threatened with a fire extinguisher by patient.
- Antique mirror removed from hallway during surgery.
- Dictaphones stolen.
- Internal thefts of petty cash.
- Script pad thefts.
- Patients urinating in waiting room.
- Abusive behaviour from patients.
- Doctor and staff cars broken into.
- Patients' coats and handbags stolen.
- Abusive behaviour when no appointments available.

Take your list and place examples against the following headings.

1   Attacks/assaults

2   Surgery thefts:

external

internal

3   Vandalising

Here you have the beginning of a risk assessment – you have begun to identify the risks. Now you need to think about what to do to minimise further events, and ensure the health and safety of everyone and everything in the practice.

What can we do?

Improve external security by introducing:

- digital locks
- an intercom system
- window locks
- alarms
- floodlights
- barbed wire surrounds.

Improve internal security by introducing:

- staff inductions
- regular staff training on dealing with aggression, assertiveness, telephone skills
- panic buttons
- restrict patients beyond certain points: put digital locks on all internal doors.

Instigate good business awareness in staff:

- keep all staff movements in a central diary so you can track the movements of everyone at all times
- keep a book in reception to sign people in and out
- keep accurate records
- maintain health and safety
- maintain your complaints policy and act on complaints immediately.

Train staff in good procedures and customer awareness:

- improve patient communications – keep patients informed through notices, newsletters and leaflets
- delight the customer
- improve services.

What are the costs of introducing these measures? Your current costs are in:

- staff and doctor morale
- repair bills
- high insurance premiums
- time.

Talk with your PCG/T about help they can give you in improving security both in their cost rent and improvement grant schemes and GP support schemes. Some PCG/Ts are introducing retainer schemes for GPs who are willing to take on and see violent patients for their colleagues locally.

Include the information you have collected in your business plan. Can you identify the areas for improvement? Can you see how this will help to improve your risk management within the practice? Include in your action plan any plans for improvement.

References

1   Quoted in *Health Service Journal*, July 2000.

2   Wilson J (1995) General practice risk management. *News for Fundholders*. **4**.

3   Lilley R and Lambden P (1999) *Making Sense of Risk Management: a workbook for primary care*. Radcliffe Medical Press, Oxford.

4   Lilley R (1999) *The PCG Tool Kit* (2e). Radcliffe Medical Press, Oxford.

5   Department of Health (1999) *The NHS Plan*. DoH, London.

6   Morris S, Willcocks G and Knasel E (1995) *How to Lead a Winning Team*. Institute of Management and Pitman, London.

7   Dr Green, Head of Risk Management, GMC. Reported in *Pulse*, December 2000.

8   Management of Health and Safety at Work Regulations 1992: Approved Code of Practice.

Further reading

Middleton J (2000) *The Team Guide to Communication*. Radcliffe Medical Press, Oxford.

For a health and safety pack for staff:

Business and Legal Reports Inc
6 Redwood
Burnham
Bucks
SL1 8JN

Tel: 01628 666166
Fax: 01628 668522

CHAPTER 8

Information management and technology (IM & T)

In this chapter we look at:

- the new developments in NHS IT
- some of the advantages and disadvantages of these developments to practices and patients
- some of the security and confidentiality issues practices need to consider in managing the risk wisely
- some of the best ways practices can use information to assist their clinical and business development.

The NHS traditionally has been good at collecting information, but not good at using it. Imagine the body of information that could be gleaned by linking prescription data to diagnosis. If this information were collated it would be used nationally to inform practice, monitor and learn from errors. This is the government plan.

The NHS Act 1999 reinforces the idea that computers will be central to delivery of healthcare in the future. The messages are not new, as the 1998 NHS Executive report Information for Health warned of changes ahead.[1] Both documents provide practices with direction and voice an integrated strategy long overdue. In addition to the £200m already invested, the government is promising an extra £250m for NHS IT development. Work is already under-way to ensure patient confidentiality issues are complied with and systems are secure. To assist this process, health authorities have set up systems for protecting and using patient information through a programme of work recommended by Caldicott. Health authorities and PCG/Ts will be assisting practices over the coming months to develop their systems to ensure they comply with this. Ask your PCG/T for more information regarding Caldicott.

Additional future plans include:

- hospital pathology results to be online by 2002
- an electronic accredited Library for Health (NELH) by 2002
- a framework for telemedicine
- GPs and suppliers to develop Read version 3 (SNOWMED clinical terms) – available in 2002.

Patients are being offered the expectation that they will be able to:

- e-mail or telephone their GP or practice nurse for advice
- book appointments online by 2005
- receive test results at home.

For healthcare staff, the following advances are proposed.

- A new system of coding to replace Read clinical terms.
- An aim to integrate GP and community patient data systems, thus abolishing the disliked Korner computer returns for all but specialised services such as mental health and maternity. The Korner data sets are now perceived to be outdated and not a useful tool for measuring activity.
- GP systems and their databases are to be accessible to other NHS institutions: A and E departments, out of hours primary care clinics, community and mental healthcare units.
- Electronic community prescribing will be introduced by 2004: prescription messages will automatically decode to the PPA (Prescription Pricing Authority) and the pharmacists.
- GPs can now rid themselves of paper systems (you need written approval for this from your health authority – this is a lengthy and costly exercise that needs resourcing).
- Video and telelinks to hospital specialists by 2005.
- Patient access to electronic personal medical records by 2004.
- Smart cards will allow lifetime patient records to be held on GP computers and by patients themselves.
- All GPs linked to NHSNet by 2002.

For the whole team

What are your views on IT?

What do you see as the advantages and disadvantages of the government plans?

What advantages do you see?

- Increased speed of communicating.
- Increased speed of processing information.
- Shared information – shared records.
- Investigations not repeated.
- More reliable information for patients, clinicians and managers.
- Linking related information, e.g. prescription with diagnosis.
- Greater efficiency.
- Easier access to the information necessary for monitoring local performance against national standards and performance indicators.

The Electronic Library of Health will enable clinicians to access the latest treatments and best practice. This primary care library aims to:

- rate the information sources it links to
- apply strict criteria of evidence base
- be relevant to primary care
- provide the right volume of information
- use accredited sources only.

Unlike Medline, its rival, a simple search for, say, migraine, will call up 28 hits, instead of Medline's 11 000 plus.[2]

What problems can we envisage?

- Resource implications.
- Increased training need and demand.
- IT can be a distraction for professionals during consultation which prevents them 'reading' the patient well.
- New work = more time.
- Inadequate communication – the medium does not allow for non-verbal clues.
- Unlike face-to-face or telephone communications, use of computers mean there is often no immediate feedback.

Implications for practices who want to develop their IT systems

 The best time to install IT is at the start-up period of the organisation's life. Otherwise IT becomes a disrespected 'add on'. IT must be seen as integral to the organisation.

Computers:

- help locate people if you operate in dual sites
- track records
- keep a record of patient encounters and 'Did not attends'
- control stock and finances
- predict re-ordering and recall times for stock, equipment and patients.

Managers like computers because of what they can do for an organisation, and luckily, technical change is often more attractive to employees than organisational change because:[3]

- computers are seen as progressive
- computers have a concrete and visible form
- workplaces with new technology are viewed in a good light by the staff
- good IT represents investment in the future and therefore job security
- computers are familiar and valued in non-work contexts.

 Most practices do not take advantage of the first year's free computer training which is generally offered with new practice systems.

This is risky behaviour. For practices who have recently invested in well recommended and networked clinical practice systems, initial training and software support is provided free. Before investing in any system, discuss your needs with your PCG/T IT support team. Their plan is usually for all their practices to have compatible systems by 2010, so that common data can be easily transferred to a central server. They will currently support systems:

- that are Read code compliant
- where data can be easily extracted and manipulated
- that can be easily expanded
- that are, or can be, networked
- that are Windows®-based
- that are accredited to their standards.

Who owns our data?

Practices need to move beyond concerns about ownership of data. Whatever management systems support primary care, there will be an increasing need to establish a reliable and coherent information base of patient related data. This information base, together with the analytical tools required to make use of the data, must provide supporting information to manage:

- Health Needs Assessment
- HImPs
- National Service Frameworks
- Performance Assessment Frameworks
- Service Agreements.

How many of the following features does your system have?

- A user interface so that you can view and enter data quickly and correctly.
- A patient reminder or recall display.
- An appointment book.
- Read codes.
- Drug codes.
- IOS claims links that allow a patient to be selected in multiple ways, e.g. name, date of birth etc.
- A pathology links module.
- A dispensing module with drug formularies.
- A portable protocol builder.
- An anatomical dictionary.
- NHSNet communications for e-mail, web browsing and structured messaging.
- A bulletin board (so you can manage your e-mails).

Does your system allow you to perform the following functions?

- Collect immunisation and screening histories.
- Use reporting and analysis tools such as MIQUEST.
- Automatically update and make visible clinical data input on all screens.
- Convert numeric data into screen graphs.
- View patient medical histories in more than one way by problem (e.g. all repeat medication) or type (medical history).
- Gain access to referral and discharge correspondence and pictures, videos, sounds and scans attached to the patient record.

Funding

For the business plan, the practice will need to note the financial implications of IT development, and who is to support the plans.

Example

The practice accepts funding for the NHSNet and associated infrastructure (messages and connection charges) will be reimbursed through being added to the standard GP remuneration package. The practice understands that health authorities and accredited regional offices are to receive additional set-up funds. It is hoped the PCT will identify additional funds for the IT planners, operational managers and data input clerks that are required within our practice to make the NHSNet implementation work.

There will be no complete prescription for primary care, as the government wants each PCG/T to write their own specification and plans; but there is an expectation that most of the day to day data collection will be done in GP practices, where the first stage of auditing can be done on small minimal data sets. Here we encounter the first problem. One of the challenges to general practice is to shift the information culture and encourage both clinicians and staff to interrogate their databases effectively – maybe giving them the protected and paid time to do so would help.

> ⟹ **For the manager**

Practices will have to put in place plans to:

* sift, sort and audit the data
* obtain information to match from trusts, consumer groups, public health and local authorities on prescribing data, epidemiological information, local trends etc.
* prepare their own health needs and health improvement analysis
* identify their needs so as to obtain sufficient funds from their locality to commission care for their patients.

Problems ahead

The problem here is both technical and cultural – money needs to be invested in practice staff to train them to meet the new needs. Time is needed to solve the problem of non-compatible and diverse GP systems, with each individual PCG/T defining compatibility. This makes out-of-area links difficult.

The strategy mentions the future need for an accredited electronic library for health, one that is owned and led by clinicians, not managers and is not management imposed. This is good, but does require big GP involvement. Managers have struggled repeatedly against a medical culture that is self-defining and does not accept outside interference. Now the strategy sets out a framework for the medical establishment to self-assess. NICE has a remit to produce and disseminate evidence-based clinical guidelines and the Commission for Health Improvement will contribute to this.

Accreditation will be crucial – there is too much unauthorised and poor quality material available at the moment. Approval by the NELH will be a welcomed addition and assist doctors who struggle with patients' self-diagnosis using poor, unstandardised self-help information now on the Internet. A spokesperson at the King's Fund notes:

'What is currently used in the NHS comes from health authorities, drug companies, patients' groups and royal colleges, and most of it is very poor quality and not worth accrediting.'[4]

These problems may be summarised as:

* technical
* financial
* training
* time.

Use of information

We recall that in 1993/4, the NHS Management Executive key strategic objectives for the NHS were to:

- improve health
- provide better services
- provide efficiency and value for money
- be organised effectively.

 At most practices, resource constraints mean there are collections of data held and not used.

One of the challenges to general practice generally is to shift the information culture and encourage both clinicians and staff to interrogate their databases effectively – giving them protected and paid time to do so would help. Accredited regional offices have received additional set-up funds for IT. Practices need to identify additional funds for the planners, operational managers and data input clerks.

It will be essential for practices to identify their needs so as to obtain sufficient funds from their locality to commission care for their patients. To be efficient and effective, the practice should be working towards a shared medical record, a common database of information required by primary care, community and acute sectors, accessible to all parties.

There is a need too to differentiate between the first generation information already collected and familiar to general practice and the new information now required.

Consider whether your practice collects the following information.

- Cytology targets.
- Breast cancer risk factors.
- CHD factors.
- Repeat scripts.
- Immunisation.
- Health promotion appointments.
- Diagnosis.

In using new information constructively, practices should be considering the following.

How is the data collected?

- ○ Is it accurate – does it reflect reality?
- ○ Is it timely – how soon after events is it made available?
- ○ Is it relevant – how related is it to the needs of those using it?

○   Is it comprehensive?
○   Is it easy to use – is it in a form that is accessible and easily manipulated?

There is no point in collecting data for the sake of it.

What sort of data do practices need to collect?

See the website for the information needs for commissioning healthcare for your population, health needs analysis and the shared medical record.

Is your practice struggling with its computer system?

As we have seen, although most practices are now computerised, most need help with data:

- management
- quality
- consistency
- coding
- searches
- audits
- analysis
- presentation
- understanding the system capabilities.

Assumptions are often made by outsiders that:

- someone in the practice knows how to retrieve data
- every practice interprets their data in the same way
- practices value the efforts made by individuals to create and maintain good systems.

But this is rare.

In recognition of the problems some practices are having, the government is supporting the Primary Care Data Quality Project (PCDQ). This project is run from a partner organisation of the NELH. Its MIQUEST software was commissioned by the NHS to allow extracted data to be:

- standardised
- anonymised
- pooled

from a variety of proprietary GP systems.

All GP systems will eventually need to be MIQUEST-compliant in order to achieve official accreditation. Many PCTs are already running pilot projects in GP practices in their area.

The PCDQ programme provides a mechanism for capturing the quality data required to support clinical governance and NSFs, initially CHD in particular. Under the new NSF guidelines, PCGs will need to build a CHD register, and ensure all their CHD patients are receiving optimised treatment. Using a set of queries written by this system, and following a data collection plan, practices are able to build their own register and monitor the treatment of their patients.

The package includes support on installation of the software and Read code training, to allow MIQUEST to operate on site in each practice. First of all, a query is run that identifies peculiar data on the practice system, e.g. men with positive cervical cytology results. Practices are then supported through a process that ensures their data systems are clean and tidy and ready to begin to input data. The data, once extracted, is transferred into proprietary software such as Excel for easily interpreted format. The tool can be run locally, at practice level, to identify which patients need clinical intervention.

For more information on MIQUEST, look at the website.

⇒ **For the manager**

Write a paragraph in your business plan about IT in your practice. For an example, *see* the website.

The NHS Executive Report A1103 *Information for Health*[1] outlines the implications for practices with particular reference to managing risk. This report demonstrates the need for many practices to improve their risk management techniques and invest in management excellence.

Confidentiality and security

Good information technology will not solve all our problems – it is the use and organisation of the information that will determine success or failure. There are still technical, administrative and training issues facing practices. These are all implications for the management of risk.

Here are some of the problems you may have identified.

- How to preserve and store records securely to ensure a risk-free environment.
- How best to use the information available.

The following table outlines some of the procedures that have to be considered, some of which will be solved through following national guidelines. But in order to reduce the risk to the organisation the wise manager will ensure the best protocols are in place.

 For the manager and partners

Has your practice considered these issues? *See* the website for some further technical and administrative considerations.

Clarity of information

If information in patient records is either absent or illegible, errors in diagnosis and treatment, and medical defence claims, can occur. A patient's record may be the principal document recording what the actual and intended care and treatment of them was, together with its outcome. For this reason they are vital to the management of any claim for negligence. Any abbreviations and symbols used must be agreed by all members of the team accessing the information. The BMA can advise further.[5]

Importance of communication

As we have seen, some of the most common factors affecting clinical negligence claims are communication breakdown, poor systems and processes and human error. Although managers cannot prevent the third, they can go a good way towards preventing the first three. Systems need to be in place to co-ordinate manual and electronic records among the practitioners, to ensure good access and accurate documentation. Evaluate the effectiveness of the methods you use or plan to use, and modify any risks you may measure.

Confidentiality

Consider the following points in relation to your practice.

- Check confidentiality:
  - make passwords personal to the individual accessing information
  - change passwords regularly

- ensure that patients cannot see or access computer information during the consultation
- identify patients by NHS number not name (this should apply to faxed as well as computer information)
- make breaches of confidentiality a contracted, disciplinary or dismissable offence.
- Hold data securely:
  - back up electronic records daily
  - check to ensure these can be re-loaded
  - hold back-ups securely and separately to the computer – in a fire-proof safe, for example
  - keep a manual record (hard copy) citing the relative roles and responsibilities of each employee
  - include a flow chart of the most frequently performed procedures (how to back up and log in and out, how to perform a simple audit, how to access clinical data etc.)
  - note within this procedure manual who has access to the computer
  - note staff roles and responsibilities
  - ensure that back-ups are signed off when completed
  - protect equipment from theft or accident
  - ensure that all those who need to, know who to call and what to do in an emergency, in the event of a computer crash or other equipment failure.
- Other checks:
  - Read clinical codes are currently mandatory – are they being used?
  - are the systems and their databases accessible to other NHS institutions: A and E departments, out of hours primary care clinics, community and mental healthcare units?
  - are prescription messages automatically decoding to the PPA (Prescription Pricing Authority) and the pharmacists?
  - do all GPs have access to NHSNet?
  - are online appointment systems set up?
  - are hospital pathology results online?
  - is the practice aware of the NELH?

Rights of access

Is the practice aware of the:

- 1988 Access to Medical Records Act
- 1984 and 1988 Data Protection Act
- Computer Misuse Act 1990?

⇒ **For the manager**

○ Do you know who your 'Caldicott Guardian' is?
○ What information are third parties entitled to see by when?
○ What can you charge for this?
○ When can doctors restrict information?
○ How do you inform patients that their medical records may be used to collect information about them? Through posters, the practice leaflet or a mail shot to all patients?
○ How do you tailor this information for those with special needs, to ensure it is accessible to all?
○ Are all staff asked routinely about their training needs around confidentiality and security as part of their annual appraisal cycle?
○ Do all contracts and induction material contain appropriate confidentiality requirements?
○ Do you set contracts for other staff who may, as part of their work for you, be required to access patient data?
○ Have you thought about, and discussed with your Caldicott Guardian, who 'owns' what data in your practice, and who has the right of access to this data?
○ Have you got protocols for sharing information?
○ Have you got a named individual within the practice who is responsible for security in the practice?
○ Do you have a security incident reporting system that is documented and understood by all staff as part of your risk assessment procedures?
○ Have you mapped all patient information flows into, around, and out of the practice, and analysed the levels of risk?

⇒ **For the whole team**

What issues would you need to consider in the event of a computer crash? What plans have you in place to manage this risk?

• Increased prescribing costs due to handwritten scripts.
• Loss of consultation and prescribing data and inability to audit reliably.
• Reduced generic prescribing rates.
• Direct infrastructure costs.
• Staff costs.
• Patient costs.

Data Protection Act (DPA) 1989

Some practices periodically make patient data available to external sources such as pharmaceutical companies, to improve clinical management. The 1998 DPA, and the Caldicott review, advise practices to improve their computer security and risk management systems. Data protection notification must cover all of the potential disclosures to third party organisations.

There are still many unresolved issues around the DPA. Practices therefore need to be aware of the legal implications in allowing external sources access to patient data, which can make them vulnerable to patient complaints. Practices need to be aware of their responsibilities and liabilities in the event of a complaint. Ask your PCG/T or Local Medical Committee (LMC) for additional guidance and clarification.

For an example of a contract, *see* the website.

Paperless practices

If your practice is considering going paperless, first think about the purposes of patient records.

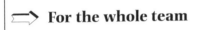 **For the whole team**

What do you need your medical record (MR) system to do? Make a note here.

Some clinical purposes

- Assist you to structure thoughts and make appropriate decisions.
- Act as an aide-memoire during subsequent consultations.

- Are available to others who are involved with the care of the same patient.
- Can store information from other parties, e.g. laboratory results.

Some non-clinical purposes

The medical records may be needed to provide:

- medico-legal evidence
- legal evidence
- evidence of workload to PCG/T
- the monitoring of services, referrals etc.

Some additional purposes

- To support teaching and/or medical education.
- To enable monitoring of possible drug side effects.
- Clinical research.

Electronic medical records (EPRs) have different characteristics. Here are some considerations; you can add your own.

Some advantages

- Can be accessed simultaneously by different people.
- Audits are easier.
- Alert warnings are improved.

Disadvantages

- Physical: EPRs require hardware and software (to be bought, maintained, upgraded, extended).
- Systems need adapting to accept remote data entry from secondary care, home visits, out of hours contacts, information from previous practice etc.
- Each practice has different electronic interfaces making data transfer problematic.
- Paper records allow for considerable freedom of expression, as codes do not reflect the breadth of normal written communication.
- Costs of implementing systems across whole practice: training, staff and infrastructure.
- Different legal characteristics have to be considered with EPRs: medical confidentiality, Caldicott, access to records etc.
- Different security aspects need to be considered with EPRs: availability, integrity, accountability, confidentiality etc.

There are coding problems to be considered:

- accurate codes need to be devised, used and understood by every user of the system
- appropriate links – between drugs and diagnoses, for example – need to be devised
- coherence in coding must be retained over time, e.g. when a diagnosed condition develops or changes or when a current problem is no longer active
- using free text to modify codes, then only the codes are recognised not the text on transfer, e.g. hysterectomy coded but not performed.

If you want to go paperless:

- apply to your PCG/T for approval
- make sure you comply with Caldicott security and confidentiality practices.

You will also need to consider:

- how you construct and use interim records for:
  - temporary residents
  - emergency treatments
  - stand-alone services, e.g. maternity or contraceptive services
- accessibility
- capacity
- storage
- the supporting hardware requirements
- your equipment needs for:
  - local or remote network support services
  - health and safety
  - security.

Some prior planning is needed

- Talk to other practices, learn from their experience.
- Make sure your system is accredited.
- Update poor quality paper records to enable them to transfer to electronic form.
- Note you will need paper and electronic access simultaneously for at least two years.
- Note the additional technologies required, e.g. a scanner.
- Develop a training and implementation policy.

Migrate slowly. Note which of your systems are currently electronically recorded:

- registration links
- IOS links

- pathology
- repeat prescriptions
- acute prescribing
- appointments
- immunisation records
- cytology records
- all investigations recorded
- basic biometrics recorded
- previous paper records summarised
- disease specific data or community medical data
- some or part consultations
- external consultations
- external text-based communications
- use of associated electronic information sources and decision support software.[6–7]

For further information on health and safety and computers, *see* the website.

References

1   NHS Executive Report (1998) *Information for Health.* The Stationery Office, London.

2   de Lusignan S (2001) Development in the NELH. *Pulse.* **2 March**: 34.

3   Daniel W and Hogarth T (1990) Worker support for technical change. *New Technology, Work and Employment.* **5**(2).

4   Coulter A (1998) King's Fund Report. *Health Service Journal.* **29 October**.

5   Anderson R (1998) *Security in Clinical Information Systems.* BMA, London.

6   NHS Executive (2000) *Electronic Patient Medical Records in Primary Care (changes to the GPs' Terms of Service).* Occasional Paper. NHSE, Leeds.

7   Joint Computing Group of the General Practitioners Committee and the Royal College of General Practitioners (2000) *Good Practice Guidelines for General Practice Electronic Patient Records. Version 2.6.* JCGGPC and RCGP, London.

Further reading

Keen J (ed.) (1994) *Information Management in Health Services.* Open University Press, Buckingham.

Further information

General Practice Risks: management and practice: www.croner.co.uk

NHS Net Library: nww.nhs.uk/nelh and www.nhs.uk/nelh

For further information on patient access to computerised records or the Code of Practice on data registration for GPs, contact the BMA office at www.bma.org.uk or:

The Data Protection Registrar
Wycliffe House
Water Lane
Wilmslow
Cheshire SK9 5AF

Tel: 01625 535777/545700

For more information on MIQUEST contact:

Anne Buckwell
Department of General Practice
St George's Hospital Medical School
London
SW17 0RE

Tel: 020 8725 5661

email: abuckwell@drs.desk.sthames.nhs.uk

CHAPTER 9

Health needs and health gain

In the wake of the recent government policy changes, it is becoming imperative for all health professionals to re-define the ways they work; otherwise they risk being left behind in the new NHS. Good practices will not only keep abreast of change but anticipate and prepare for it. We already know that part of this is:

- being proactive
- anticipating change
- modifying behaviours
- modifying ways of working to fit new demands.

Needs assessment, which looks at the needs of the population served, is one way of ascertaining new base lines from which to work. It provides a framework for all health workers to redefine their position within healthcare delivery. This applies to both clinicians and managers.

In this section, we look at some useful approaches to profiling and health needs assessment.

Some advantages of health needs assessment

- Can equip the practice with working models that may help to provide the evidence required to re-evaluate their work.
- Provides information to prioritise the service they provide.
- Profiling often reveals other needs within the organisation, such as training or resource deficits.

A good health needs analysis demonstrates that the organisation is thinking through the viability of their business. It forms an essential part of the business planning process, which in itself is crucial to managing risk.

We address:

- methods of data collection
- analysis
- resulting changes or strategies
- the strengths and weaknesses of each approach.

Needs assessment requires:

- commitment and support throughout the organisation
- liaison with the public, other professionals and policy makers: commissioners, purchasers, secondary care colleagues, attached staff and service users.

 Can you say you have already built up these necessary networks? If not, begin to now.

Needs assessment is becoming increasingly complex, and the aid of public health and epidemiologists is becoming essential; but it is possible for a even a small health organisation such as general practice to make a start at understanding their patient profile.

What is health needs assessment?

Basically, a needs assessment outlines what needs to be addressed to improve the health of a population. Broadly, it addresses the needs of the population served.
It involves:

- collecting information
- determining appropriate priorities for the health and social care of patients
- compiling a health profile of the population
- analysis of the data to assess and prioritise strategies for change.

Are you aware of all the proposals to meet the new NHS Act 1999 standards on improving health and reducing inequality? Are you aware of the clinical priorities set?

 For the doctors and manager

Outline your proposals to meet any national or local standards, regulations or guidelines.

- Do you know about the national priority groups selected for investment and reform?

○   Do you know your local priority groups for action?
○   What is your own priority group, if it differs?
○   How is the practice going to organise itself to meet the new guidance?

The NHS Plan has brought some new national priorities – look at the website for these, and for an example template.

Practices must start to put a plan in place to collect all the necessary information required to meet these new government targets. Forward thinking practices will already be doing some of this work and will be aware that it is just this kind of work that will meet any new clinical governance standards.

  For the manager

Begin by collecting information about the patients in your practice. Which of the following can you start collecting already?

• A computer-generated list of diagnoses.
• A computer list of operations performed.
• A consultation data log.
• Referral data analysis.
• Morbidity or mortality details.
• Information about any local factors likely to have an impact on health.

In health needs analysis, either at practice or locality level, the following types of information will need collecting. This is good management use of clinical information, and it is where audit comes in.

Information needs in understanding and commissioning healthcare for your population

• Facts about your population – pockets of deprivation, spread within the district, by council ward or postcode area.
• Health status of the population – lifestyle risks, common complaints. This will give you a broad picture of the disease patterns in the area you are working in, and an indication of resource needs.
• Note and agree targets for the health status of your population: for example, do you want 70% of your practice population to be non-smoking by the year 2005?
• Establish information and agree targets for existing services offered. For example, 65% of the women aged between 55 and 65 currently take up the breast screening offered; the new target is 70% by 2002.
• Establish variances in local services – using waiting list and league table information provided by trusts and health authorities.

- Establish the consequences of these variances – this needs to be a political and public debate where a judgement is made between, say, funding cancer or heart disease services.
- Decide possible interventions: audit, challenge old practices, keep up to date with research and opinion, re-audit and evaluate.
- Identify costs and benefits if possible – use provider and practice information. Learn to measure benefits in terms of increased health (discuss the parameters with practitioners and local authority colleagues). These may be physical, social, mental or emotional health gains as well as lack of disease. The gains may not always be clearly identifiable as financial, but measured in decrease in uptake of a service, for example.
- Produce an action list of the proposed changes which should increase benefit or reduce cost.
- Review and reassess the impact made.

Information needs for health needs analysis

- Demographic data (age/sex/census data) available from the GP practice age/sex register.
- Birth and death information – available through public health and OPCS codes.
- Morbidity data about illness and disability from recent census, practice databases and disability registrations.
- Services used – using primary care, health authority, social services and trust minimum data sets.

In general practice, good needs assessment could help prevent a situation where partners only pick up the work they like, although of course, currently patients can choose a practice for its specialties. This may change as PCTs organise work on a locality basis; then community needs assessment really comes into its own. Practices will therefore need to assess current provision and review the skills necessary to meet patients' needs. Without this, the organisation is at risk of being unable to meet the demands made of it. It is a user-driven process not a professional one, as PCTs will be looking for the number of GP posts to directly correlate to the number of patients in need, not to be inflated through professional demand.

For our purposes, we will look at the information that needs collecting at practice level, as this should be readily obtainable and can easily be collated for group analysis. We are working on the common assumptions that:

- GPs are in a key position for information gathering
- the majority of health episodes occur in primary care
- 98% of the population see their GP every 3–5 years
- information gathered is broad spectrum

- general practice is humanistic
- GP diagnoses cover physical, psychological and social aspects.

It is a complex process. A picture of health is created through:

- epidemiology
- morbidity data
- mortality data
- locality analysis
- demographics
- auditing and evaluation of current and historical activity
- review of current medical opinion and the evaluation of clinical outcomes.

What is *need?*

The definition of *need* is interpreted personally, depending on political, personal and professional contexts. Generally, it is felt the focus should be on the client. Here, we look at one interpretation.

- Normative needs – defined by professionals according to their standards.
- Felt needs – perceived by an individual or a community.
- Expressed needs – when felt needs progress to a demand.
- Comparative needs – defined when one community becomes aware that another community has a service or resource that the first desires.[1]

How do we analyse the health of our practice population?

Group methods

One method is for practices to group together to share clinical data to provide useful epidemiological data. This can be conducted as part of the clinical governance process: to improve clinical practice and as an educative process or part of the audit cycle. It can also be used to inform the commissioning processes. In the process described below, individual practices may download anonymised Read code consultation data on to a central PCG/T or health authority database from which a current picture of morbidity could be ascertained.

⟹ **For the doctors and manager**

Use the following as a checklist.

Training

- Prior to sending out the data, staff will need additional training in coding.
- Training could be provided by computer software companies, health authority IT department or local medical audit advisory group (MAAG).
- Can your computer software run checks to flag up odd or unusual diagnoses and those incompatible with the patient's age and sex?

Communication

Practices must agree on:

- common clinical definitions of conditions
- the quality of the data
- data compatibility.

Broad communication should occur across the whole primary healthcare team, as individual groups of staff may have a lot to contribute in the area of needs assessment, particularly community nurses, who have to conduct these profiles as part of their post-basic training.

Use of information

Amalgamated data could be used to check:

- the number of surgical procedures performed locally against the national average incidence
- whether there are wide variations in consultation rates for particular diagnoses across surgeries
- intra-practice, inter-practice and national variations in incidence and diagnosis of a given pathology.

Individual methods

An easier method is for a single practice to look more closely at something the practice feels is a problem, such as a rise in teenage pregnancies or suicide admissions. Your local MAAG or HImP programme could help inform the process. The assessment will help the practice identify whether the problem is bigger than average, and act as a pointer to solutions. Prior to collecting the data, some questions need consideration.

Resources

Can you compare your practice needs with another, local, one as a comparison? It is hard to make a case of need if you are unable to prove comparative hardship. You may need to enlist the help of another practice, or the PCG/T on this.

Evidence

Is there good evidence for the effectiveness of treatment for the group of patients you have identified? Use national or local protocols to help define this, or Royal College or NICE guidelines.

Outcomes

Are there measurable outcomes to enable you to judge the effectiveness of your interventions? Ask your local MAAG for help here.

Use of information

Using the information, you may be able to answer some questions such as whether or not you are getting the best payments for the service you provide for both your patients and your staff.

- Are you getting a fair share of the national and local resource?
- Does your practice best fit its service to the needs of these patients?
- Are there any areas where you need to take a different approach?

Review the data and compare with national and local demographic information by keeping abreast of information on the outside influences on your organisation e.g. socio-psychological forces, legal and political influences and economic trends.

Data to collect

Use this information to map a bigger profile of your practice population. You can use it to inform or add to the earlier part of your business plan. Is the practice expecting any hardware or software updates that would enable this information to be gathered more readily?

Audit the characteristics of the practice population through:

- Level 3 PACT data analysis (available from the PPA). If you have a practice or local formulary, this must be reviewed
- disease registers
- referral analysis (from April 2001 this has been a NHS Act 1999 requirement)

- Read diagnosis codes
- Read consultation codes.

Look specifically at:

- cause of death
- social class distribution
- age/sex register
- ethnic origins of patients
- number of advantaged and disadvantaged people such as those in full time employment, lone parents, homeless, travellers, the economically inactive and the elderly living alone
- mortality rates including deaths from heart disease, suicide, cancer and accidents
- morbidity rates including occurrence rates of chronic conditions such as asthma, diabetes and chronic mental illness
- number of children on child protection register
- stress factors: poverty, unhealthy environments etc.
- other problems local to you: alcohol abuse, drug addiction etc.

See if you can compare these figures against national and local demographic analysis, such as local census material provided by the local authority or council.

Note any other audit needs, e.g.:

- body mass index
- blood pressure readings
- history of coronary heart disease
- history of stroke/transient ischaemic attack
- smear and immunisation data
- other disease groups given a local priority.

Run the audit cycle: test, analyse and review data, make recommendations and then re-test.

Some ideas on what to audit within particular patient groups (add your own):

- numbers seen annually
- numbers not seen
- variations from original proposals
- planned changes
- appointment availability
- admission rates
- re-attendance rate
- types of consultation
- avoidable deaths.

Local factors impacting on health

- Chart which areas your patients live in – affluent or deprived?
- What is the local pollution index?
- What are the local economic conditions for example: the housing stock, the leisure facilities, food supplies, employment availability and public transport facilities? Build up a picture of your surroundings.

For an example of an individual practice analysis, *see* the website.
   You would need to include:

- prevalence analysis
- practice consultation and referral rates
- morbidity data
- expected treatment outcomes
- recommendations
- needs analysis.

 Supporting documents: make the evidence to support your claims graphic and clear: use tables, pie charts or histograms for best effect.

 For the doctors and manager

Note the problems with this sort of exercise.

- Problem of small sample sizes in general practice.
- Who can we compare data with? Where can we find practices with similar enough patient profiles to compare with?
- What other variables do we need to consider?

Reference

1   Bradshaw J (1992) The concept of social need. *New Society*. **30**: 640–3.

CHAPTER 10

Audit

'How many times does a member of staff have to be rude to a patient before it is statistically significant?'

Sue Lister[1]

 Practices need to build audit into their management structure and develop a culture that accepts audit as an essential multi-disciplinary or whole team activity.

Is audit going out of fashion?

Medical, clinical and administrative audit was made popular in the early 1990s, as a risk management tool that was also clinically and managerially useful. This still stands, although the popularity of medical audit has waned in recent years, with the stress moving away from medical audit towards multi-disciplinary or whole team audit activities. The reasons for this are cultural and practical: the emerging consensus within the NHS is that *'real improvement can only take place through changes to systems and organisation of care, rather than changing individual working practice.'*[1]

Why is this?

- Clinicians (doctors in particular) hold out against central regulation in general, preferring internal professional self-regulation.
- Few doctors feel financial or managerial issues affect their decision making in any way.
- Knowledge obtained through audit tends to remain hidden among professionals.
- Knowledge is rarely transferred to the organisation as a whole.

These sentiments have prompted the recent decision to bring decision making into a management and organisational framework.

- NICE will undertake their own audits and publish their recommendations nationally.
- The NHS Act 1999 recommends that PMS contracted practices – and, it is likely, all practices – will have to undertake up to three audits annually.

The background to medical audit is important as it leads the way into the medical profession understanding some of the terms, uses and definitions used by managers in administrative audit. Managers find audit one of the most useful of their managerial tools. Many practice managers in primary care take the lead in preparing the ground for audit in their practices: clinical audit is not exclusively medical. It may well involve all members of the healthcare team, patients and other care workers in looking at any aspect of clinical care.

The benefits of audit

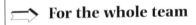 **For the whole team**

Mark off which of the following gains you feel would be useful to your practice.

For the partners

Audit:

- is a simple, effective and low cost way of sifting and analysing data
- aims to promote higher standards of care, effectiveness and efficiency
- integrates modern practice into the management structure
- is a prerequisite for, and secures, effective medical defence
- reduces risk by allowing a team to identify and eliminate areas of potential hazard before a mistake is made
- saves money
- provides information about current practice
- helps to improve standards of care
- highlights any discrepancies between perceived standards of practice and measured standards
- is intrinsically rewarding, as it measures improvement
- aids in bidding for resources
- stimulates education.

For the organisation

Audit is being encouraged by lead organisations (the NHS Executive, training bodies, local and regional health authorities and academic institutions). To be seen to undertake audit regularly puts your organisation in a good light; it shows the organisation is keen to:

- critically analyse its performance
- improve its performance
- enhance its accountability
- demonstrate awareness of personal responsibility for its actions
- give a clear and full explanation of its activities to external agencies including patients, policy makers, senior managers or colleagues
- improve effectiveness
- improve efficiency
- demonstrate sound management principles. It is no coincidence that the audit cycle closely follows the management cycle.

For the manager and staff

- Makes work systems more efficient, cost effective, and stress free.
- Gives a structure around which to identify and work out a programme of change.
- Encourages problems to be aired and shared.
- Encourages a critical and analytical look at the practice.
- Those taking part see it as a less threatening, constructive criticism.
- Encourages team discussion and decision making rather than management led change.
- Aids decision making.
- Is empowering – teams can use audits to work out change themselves.
- Is educative.

What is audit?

Audit is an objective and systematic way of evaluating the quality of care or service delivery. There are various terms used to describe the audit of healthcare, with which we are concerned.

1 **Medical audit** concerns the performance of doctors and their professional competence.
2 **Clinical audit** evaluates an aspect of clinical care provided by any members of the health organisation.
3 **Administrative audit** or **internal audit** is the audit of activities by non-medical staff, using criteria defined by the organisation itself.

4   **External audit** is carried out by outsiders, using criteria defined by
    authorities outside the organisation.
5   **Self audit** is conducted by individuals or a group within the practice.
6   **Peer audit** is where several practices get together to compare their audit
    findings.

Is audit research?

This is debatable. It does use some research tools (data collection and analysis)
but is not tied to research methodology. Scientific research methods are about
proving facts in a way that can be replicated by other people using the same
method.

Audit is different. The aim of internal audit, which we look at here, is to
examine a particular practice and see whether it can be done better – nobody
else's practice is relevant. Audit does not require a hypothesis, a control group
or a statistically significant sample (although the data collection does need to
provide the audit team with enough information to be convincing).

The audit cycle

Audit involves a sequence of steps that include:

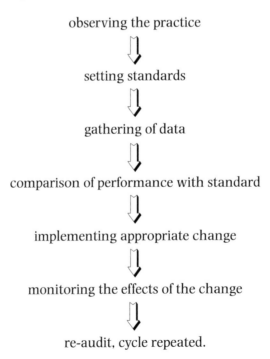

observing the practice

setting standards

gathering of data

comparison of performance with standard

implementing appropriate change

monitoring the effects of the change

re-audit, cycle repeated.

Traditionally these steps are illustrated by a circular diagram; as a sequence of steps that can be started at any point and taken in any order. The steps, when repeated, give audit a cyclical quality.

What can be audited?

Audit works best when a group of people decide on something to investigate and improve – ownership of the audit is important.

⇒ **For the whole team**

What needs improvement in your practice:

○ a service?
○ a building design?
○ a way of working?
○ a method of recording?
○ a way of organising?

When do you audit? The example given by Sue Lister is enlightening: '*How many times does a member of staff have to be rude to a patient before it is statistically significant?*' Audit now.

Traditionally, management audit is concerned with two components – structure and process. Structure can include the material environment and process examines service delivery.

Here are the structures and processes that one practice wanted to look at.

Categorise the following items by type: financial, clinical or organisational

- Buildings
- Equipment
- Staff qualifications
- Number of staff
- The frequency of a diagnosis recorded in the notes
- Monitoring access and availability through appointment systems
- Number and categories of telephone calls into the practice
- Referral and prescribing patterns
- Use and adherence to pre-agreed protocols and clinical procedures
- Case note analysis
- Peer review

- Survey
- Significant event analysis.

Financial	Clinical	Organisational

Some audit examples

The following examples demonstrate the versatility and use of audit to measure and change practice and demonstrate its use as a resource management tool.

Practice A: patient satisfaction questionnaire

This audit looked at a group of patients' views of surgery times, appointment availability, waiting times and demand for clinics at a GP surgery. As a result of the responses received, standards were set on waiting times for routine appointments. The practice is currently reassessing the need for advertising some of their clinics, and is using these results to modify how it publicises services.

Practice B: staffing

This health centre looked at skill mix and the minimum cover required to run the practice efficiently. A plan was produced which radically altered the staffing structure and reallocated responsibilities. This plan went out to the staff and partners for consultation, and was substantially modified. As a result, first line staff management responsibilities were devolved, reception staff were redeployed to take on some of the practice nurse administration, and the reception telephone was reallocated.

Practice C: nursing

There were conflicting ideas in this practice about the role of practice nurses. This skill mix review looked at nursing activity (clinical, administrative and other tasks) over a set time, and also examined the diagnostic groups seen in that time. From this, waiting time standards were set, the drop-in facility was changed to an appointment system and administrative tasks were devolved to lower graded staff. The nursing job descriptions were re-defined to include higher managerial and clinical responsibilities.

Practice D: paediatric and mental health referrals

This group of GPs were analysing their referral rates across various specialties. They wished to compare the actual number of referrals across the practice with a predicted assumed annual growth of 3%. The practice used this data to demonstrate to their PCT that their annual referral growth rates to these two specialists were managed and reasonable, and that the assumed growth rates were based on list size growth not inflation. This practice also audited and analysed referral rates by doctor, and used the results to set standards for clinical protocols.

How to audit

 For the whole team

As a team, think about how you could audit access and availability through appointment systems.

○ How could you find out if patients were being prioritised according to pre-agreed criteria for referral?
○ How could you find out the time of arrival, time of appointment and time seen?
○ How could you find out when the next available appointment is?
○ Would you want to look at this by clinical speciality or on a named basis?
○ What are the shortfalls to this approach and what are the influencing factors the practice needs to note?

The audit

Pre-audit

• Hold a meeting with all relevant personnel.
• Establish and agree the need for the audit.
• Use everyone who has an involvement with the system or procedure being analysed.
• Choose topics that inspire and interest people.
• Find out why staff do not wish to take part – is training required? If so, set it up.

- Set up your audit so staff are able to carry it out with minimal support or effort.
- Give the audit a title that reflects the complexity of the subject.

Meet with all relevant personnel to establish and agree the need for and title of the audit. If possible, this should involve everyone who has an involvement with the system or procedure being analysed. Not only is this good management, but the more people involved the more creative the suggestions.

If the topics chosen do not inspire, find out why. If staff require training, most PCG/Ts have medical audit advisors or facilitators who would be happy to assist.

Although audit can technically be done manually, using an age/sex register for example, or trailing through patient notes, there are immense advantages in using IT for audits. It is quicker and simpler to make use of IT, either using the printed lists of data that most clinical systems used by GPs churn out, or preferably, a database such as Microsoft Access.

The case study

Use this case study to compare how you conduct your audits.

The problem

GP practice X was having a problem with their telephone system. There were many complaints from both patients and outside professionals that the telephone lines were constantly engaged. Reports were that the call stacking system sounded a ringing tone so users of the service felt no one was answering. There was one switchboard operator and this job was rotated due to its unpopularity, as the callers were often irritated or abusive. The practice was beginning to lose its reputation and patients.

The audit title

'To investigate the number and type of telephone calls into GP practice X, when they occur and who responds. To develop a more cost effective and efficient system to deal with the variety of calls.'

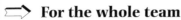 **For the whole team**

Here are come considerations.

Criteria and standards

Aspects of care or procedures can only be measured if there is an objective or standard to compare it with. With new audits, agree standards on the basis of what the group considers good practice. Have you set your standards using:

o   studies?
o   previously published audits?
o   locally agreed practice?

Donabedian defined a criterion as '*a set of discrete, clearly definable and measurable phenomena... that are in some specifiable way relevant to the definition of quality*'.[2]
   Have you used this stage to:

o   set ideal standards, the best attainable in the best conditions?
o   consider cost and compromise later, when the group revisits the audit to examine how change is to be implemented?
o   use measurable, qualitative and quantitative objectives, for example: 'a 20% reduction in complaints by x, y number of calls to be answered within z minutes'?
o   be as clear and specific as possible?

An *explicit criterion* is one that is declared and written down. An *implicit criterion* is one that:

•   uses personal experience and knowledge
•   may assess attitudes
•   may assess subtle variations in care
•   uses values that may be spoken but not written.

Criteria can be *external*, i.e. chosen by those outside the audit, for example professional colleagues, societies etc.) or *internal*, i.e. external standards that have been readjusted to suit the audit team. These are the most successful as they meet the particular needs of the people in practice:

1   80% of calls into the practice should be answered within ten seconds
2   the practice aims for a 50% reduction in complaints over a three month period.

Methodology

•   Decide and note your methods of data collection.
•   Note the type of audit you are undertaking.
•   Note if your data collection will be manual or computer.

- Devise the data collection form.
- Cost up the staff time to collect and analyse the data.

A confidential enquiry is a term often used to describe a significant event audit, where data is collected with an aim to identify the circumstances leading to adverse or unusual events.[3] This is often used in general practice as a review of individual cases.

Data collection

Is your data:

- a collection of facts
- a set of observations
- a set of measurements?

Although the amount of data does not need to be statistically significant (*see* p. 206, Is audit research?), make certain enough data is selected to make the audit convincing.

Sampling

Are your samples:

- selected so that inferences about that group of people, events or objects can be made using relevant sample data? For example, if you have a specific age/sex/ethnic bias to your population, your sample must represent this.
- selected with a predisposition towards one particular view which will distort the results?
- selected randomly, systematically, or as a one-off?

Generally, however, the size of the sample is immaterial. What is important is that the practice or audit team needs to be convinced of the representation and relevance of the data presented to them.

Types of sampling

It is important to have a representative sample of the population. In order to reduce bias, it may be necessary to sample at random. This is especially important in retrospective data collection, where random sampling facilitates valid sampling. This reduces the opportunity to select particular examples from memory. The best random samples are generated using random numbers taken from a computer.

For the whole team

Are you familiar with the following terms?

- Sequential samples
- Stratified random sample
- Representative sampling
- Systematic sample
- Random case analysis.

Sequential samples: when cases are taken in their original order.
Stratified random sample: where distinct sub-groups are identified then random samples are drawn from each.
Systematic sample: where you start at an arbitrary point in a list and choose cases at regular intervals after that.
Random case analysis: often used as a teaching tool in medical audit, where the case of a particular patient is chosen at random.

The sample size

How many clinics or surgeries do you have to observe to confirm a trend that patients are waiting longer than is acceptable?

Most managers will have a gut feeling here – five complaints in a year of 2500 surgeries is probably acceptable, but 20% is not. The team can improve their accuracy using simple mathematics.

If, for example, the audit were to assess how many patients had their blood pressure taken in the last year, a sample of 15 patients out of a list of 2000 would not give you enough detail. To be accurate, the audit needs to assess 100% of the records, but to be 95% certain (+ or – 5%) 325 sets need to be examined if the list size is 2000 patients. The only time the audit needs to examine 100% of the records is if it is to ascertain the number of patients missed – using the above example, all the hypertensives who have not been seen.

- Have you defined your population?
- Is your sample complete?
- Is it representative?
- Is it relevant and valid?
- Is it confidential?
- Have you identified your sample type?

When handling data the manager needs to consider what methods of storage and protection they use as well as the way they manipulate or analyse the data. The way the data is understood is influenced by the choice of presentation in reporting.

Audit requires the gathering of objective data, and this objectivity may be affected by the method of data collection.

 For the whole team

Some more terms:

- retrospective audits
- enhanced records
- prospective audit.

Retrospective audits:

- review records to gather facts about past activities
- examine existing records whose data may be incomplete
- make judgements only on what actually is recorded
- overcome bias by planning to collect data prospectively.

Enhanced records:

- are elaborated clinical records which allow consistent comparison and effective future prospective audit.

Prospective audit:

- is the process of gathering data as it happens
- usually takes place over a prescribed and defined period of time
- usually uses a pre-determined number of cases
- has advantages in that the data completeness can be controlled
- usually uses purpose-designed data collection forms (recording sheets) or computerised data entry.

What can you see as the disadvantage of prospective audit?

Participants may be tempted to alter data to meet a personal agenda, bringing in a research bias.

For an example of a prospective audit, *see* the website.

Check for confidentiality

All health service workers are signed up to an ethical duty to keep information about patients private and confidential. Any staff member handling data has a duty not to disclose learned sensitive information to any third party. The General Medical Council (1993) have allowed that information may be disclosed with the explicit consent of the patient. However, in the case of audit, the general rule is that anonomised data should be used where possible. If at any stage a disclosure would enable an individual patient to be identified, that person must be informed and advised of their right to withold consent to disclosure.

Do you:

○ obtain consent from patient if necessary?
○ anonomise patient information?
○ avoid codes that could identify patients or doctors?
○ destroy audits when complete?
○ register with the Data Protection Act?

Analyse the data

Comparing the observed practice with the standards set

Use your data to answer as many questions put to it as possible. You may wish to use the data to answer linked questions, e.g.:

○ How many women complained compared to men?
○ When was the peak time for callers in this sample?
○ When was the slackest time?
○ Which GP had the most calls?
○ Did the caller's sex reflect your list profile?
○ How does the data collected compare with your standards set?

Note the measured differences and use your analysis to discuss and implement any change required.

Presentation

Methods of presentation influence the observer's understanding or interpretation of the material. Using a spreadsheet such as Microsoft Excel radically improves your presentation of findings:

 For the whole team

What is the preferred method for looking at frequency of occurrence?

A histogram or frequency polygon.

What is the preferred method for looking at the contribution of each value to the total?

Pie charts.

What is the preferred method for comparing (a) with (b)?

Bar charts compared across categories.
   It may be useful for the team to recall some statistical terms:

- the mode is the most frequently occurring item or number
- the mean is the (mathematical) average
- the median is the middle value in a series of numerical values arranged in order of magnitude.

Evaluation

After the material has been prepared for presentation, the audit group will evaluate the information. Here they gather together all the information for the purpose of making a judgement about its acceptability.

Setting standards and implementing change

- Discuss with all parties.
- Remember ownership of standards.
- Take care to exclude bias when measuring, analysing, interpreting and displaying the data.
- Make the presentations readable and exciting: use graphic displays and summaries where possible.

Use the data to engender discussion with all parties involved. Ownership of standards is a vital stage in accepting the validity of an audit, even though the technical side may have been carried out by others. All aspects of the audit need to be of personal relevance.
   Ask yourself the following questions.

- Is the present standard of care satisfactory? It may be that the practice decides a 60-second answering delay is acceptable, and does not change anything.
- How can things be altered to achieve better results?
- Do the standards need to be reset?
- What are your minimum and optimum standards.

In this example, the practice decided to make some major changes to their telephone system based on the complaints alone. The discussion engendered some new, preferred standards that the practice wanted to set for their telephone system. These would form the basis for re-audit within the year, and the basis for discussion with the telephone company providing the service. The audit results were used as a base line for discussion with the local health authority, who were happy to contribute towards a new telephone system and part time receptionist who could staff a stand-alone results line.

Quality

Additional new standards were set:

1 all incoming calls should be routed to the relevant person at second or third access via a touch tone system
2 callers should be informed of their place in a stacking system
3 unstacked calls should sound an engaged tone
4 emergency/duty calls should be routed to a live operator at the first or second access point. Note: it is a legal and statutory requirement that a patient calling a doctor in an emergency should be given a staffed number (second call) so any 999 call will be the third number called
5 doctors should retain protected lines, extension numbers given out only with GP permission
6 switchboard operators must be given clear written guidelines on how to deal with abusive clients and emergency (life threatening) calls.

Outcome

Outcome may be defined as the result or visible effect of an event.[4] Donabedian's definition applies more aptly to health:

> 'A change in the patient's current and future health status that can be attributed to antecedent healthcare.'[2]

In clinical audit, there needs to be some measurable relationship to a process performed on a patient. However, as we know, either positive or negative outcome can occur as a result of a whole range of environmental and lifestyle influences, not all of which are under clinical control. Thus the term *health outcome* may be better used, to describe the result of one or more health interventions.

For the doctors

Can you describe your intervention process clearly – who did what to whom?

What terms would you use to measure changes in health status?

In medicine, health status may be measured in the following terms:

- biomedical control
- symptom level
- functional status
- psychosocial status
- patient satisfaction
- increased knowledge
- behaviour changes.

If health change does occur as a result of your interventions, it is hard to be objective about the measurement of this change – could the change be reduplicated? How reliable is it? Is it valid? Lohr, in 1998 said that 'outcomes can be short term, long term or anything in between, and the classifications can be quite arbitrary.'[5] She suggested that criteria could be measured more accurately through defining:

- purpose (individual patients, populations or similar patients)
- source of information (patients, carers or medical records)
- mode of data collection (interviews, questionnaires or medical records)
- agent responsible for interpretation (provider, manager or policy maker).

The comparision of outcomes across or between services is known as *outcome benchmarking*.

Reassess

Reassessment is often termed 'closing the loop'. It should be defined how soon reassessment should occur. The audit group will then begin again to monitor the effect of the changes in place, adjust practice in the light of results, quantify the improvement in the standards of care and repeat the survey to test for evidence of effective change.

> ⟹ **For the team**

What do you see as the disadvantages of audit?

Some common answers

- Time.
- Money – data analysis and collection both time consuming; own database needed to make it cost effective.
- Measuring standards against other national or local standards – not available.
- Need to remember to rerun audits – mark in diary next year. New is always more exciting to a creative non-finisher.

Management tools required

Audit is a systematic management tool: a way of analysing data that follows a complete cycle of preparation, standard setting, analysis, change and evaluation. It is a research tool but one that does not require much academic or intellectual input – audit is practical and easy, with formal, well documented stages to assist those new to it.

A manager who leads or co-ordinates an audit will be expected to be creative, able to provide new ideas and able to translate plans into action. They would need to be familiar with national clinical audit governance/effectiveness guidelines. Ideally their skills base would show:

- a wide range of general management skills
- good interpersonal skills
- good communication skills
- numeracy and literacy
- computer literacy: knowledge of spreadsheets, for example, Microsoft Excel; knowledge or use of data analysis packages, for example, Microsoft Access; and word processing skills.

 **For the team**

Do the GPs and nurses in your practice:

○ advocate and support audit
○ make resources available for audit
○ adhere to any changes implemented?

Does the manager:

○ organise audit so that it is a systematic activity
○ feedback results to all staff
○ encourage team involvement
○ compare results with other practices?

Does everyone in the practice (nurses, receptionists and attached staff):

○ suggest topics
○ take part
○ feedback to colleagues
○ help by gathering data
○ reinforce changes by reminding others about new systems?

Most practices are familiar with clinical audits which evaluate an aspect of clinical care, e.g. smear adequacy, lithium monitoring, first year diphtheria, tetanus and polio boosters and influenza vaccine. Many are not yet familiar with administrative or internal audit, which look at activities by non medical staff, using criteria defined by the organisation itself, e.g. practice nurse activity audit. Some practices have been scrutinised by an external audit, using criteria defined by PCGs or the health authority.

Nervous practices could begin by undertaking a structural audit on number and skills of staff, and a process audit which examines, for example, referral and prescribing patterns. Medical audit, which concerns the performance of doctors and their professional competence, is still rarely undertaken in practices. The clinical governance agenda hopes to address this.

References

1   Lister S (1995) Statistics and audit: not necessarily correlated. *Audit in General Practice*. **3**(3).

2   Donabedian A (1980) The definition of quality: a conceptual exploration. In: A Donabedian (ed.) *Explorations in Quality Assessment and Monitoring*. University of Michigan, Ann Arbor.

3   Bradley CP (1992) Turning anecdotes into data: the critical incident technique. *Family Practice.* **9**: 98–103.

4   Brown L (ed.) (1993) *New Shorter Oxford English Dictionary.* Clarendon Press, Oxford.

5   Lohr KN (1988) Outcome measurement: concepts and questions. *Inquiry.* **25**: 37–50.

Further reading

Samuel O, Grant J and Irvine D (1999) *Quality and Audit in General Practice: meanings and definitions.* RCGP, London.

PART THREE

CHAPTER 11

Staff roles and responsibilities

This section deals with the professional requirements needed to manage staff. We look at staff roles and responsibilities within the practice, staff management, human resource management and some of the issues that impact on good management within the practice: training and professional development, leadership styles, communication styles and motivation. We complete the section by looking towards the future and at the management techniques used to manage change successfully.

In this chapter, we look at the essential procedures – job descriptions, employment contracts etc. that you would expect all practices to have in place. In the following three chapters we look in more detail at the broader functions of personnel management.

'If Florence Nightingale were carrying her lamp through the corridors of the NHS today, she would most certainly be searching for the people in charge.'

Sir Roy Griffiths

General practice as a whole recognises that its staff are its most valuable asset and are also the most expensive. However, most practices do not regularly review their staff roles and responsibilities, so there is no base line from which to develop and cost the skills available within the practice. In many practices, for example, nurses spend too much time ordering and monitoring stock. They are often solely responsible for clinical computer input and editing notes, but other, and cheaper, members of staff could take these roles on if trained. In most practices, jobs have evolved over time and the best person has not always been found for the job needed. In November 2000 the government announced a review of the entire NHS workforce, to evaluate roles and responsibilities to be completed by 2004.

 Practices should undertake regular skill mix reviews and have to hand documented staff profiles demonstrating key staff skills and any training needs.

For the manager

The manager needs to include a staff profile in the business plan which includes:

- the names of staff
- their whole time equivalent hours worked
- their job title, grade and pay per hour
- a brief synopsis of the skills held
- any training needs.

You will then be in a position to undertake a skill mix review.

- Be ruthless, honest and objective
- Do this job in absolute confidence, do not disclose your findings to anyone until the job is complete.

So:

- map out the key skills and hours required against the available skills and hours
- map out the required tasks
- note any discrepancies
- match those best suited and graded for the job required
- identify when the job would be best done.

You may find that a receptionist has proved herself to have brilliant analytical and VDU skills, and would be best placed to take on a responsible auditing role. You may find the highest paid person in the practice is a medical secretary, who can in fact only undertake audio typing. You may find that all the reception staff work school hours and you are paying overtime for the night surgery filing.

Look realistically at what the job needs. Then:

- discuss the findings with the partners
- discuss the findings with the staff individually at staff appraisals

It will not be possible to make all changes immediately, but earmark job changes when staff leave and you need to replace them.

 Always use the opportunity when staff change to re-jig the job to the hours and tasks that best suit the practice. There will be resistance to this, so stand firm!

Workforce planning

The NHS Plan (HR Strategy *Working Together*) makes a requirement for PCG/Ts and ultimately practices to consider how they are going to meet the needs of changing clinical demands. One way to address this is by workforce planning. Basically, this means thinking through the key issues that need to be considered when planning ahead to meet the needs of your population.

Workforce planning:

- needs to be linked to the local HImP
- should support plans to develop your services
- should cover all staff groups
- should be focused on changes in service levels and delivery patterns.

Although such planning may seem time consuming, the main benefits arising from forward planning in this way are that:

- PCGs will thank you for helping them to meet their target to have an annual workforce plan in place
- practices will be better placed and informed when applying against the GMS bidding process for more ancillary staff funds
- practices will be better prepared if staff shortages hit
- plans will be directly related to service developments.

How to plan?

> ⇒ **For the whole team**

Use the following disease groups:

- cancer
- coronary heart disease
- mental health
- older people's services
- children's services
- intermediate care/rehabilitation/primary care
- any new NSFs.

GPs and practice nurses should consider:

- which treatments occur in primary care
- who is involved in the patient pathways

- which of these staff groups is now, or may in future, be employed in primary care
- what the skills required are
- what the evidence base is
- if there is anyone else who could provide the same service
- what training and supervision they would require
- what the predicted delivery models are
- how these new models affect staffing numbers/roles/working arrangements
- what the foreseen impacts of new technology/treatments are.

Did you consider all staff groups?

- From primary care:
  - GPs
  - nurses
  - non-clinical staff (manager and receptionists)
  - counsellors.
- From the community trust or social services:
  - occupational therapists
  - physiotherapists
  - speech and language therapists
  - psychology
  - community nurses.

⇒ **For the manager**

- Review the current staff and service provision.
- Make a chart specifying current workforce numbers, grades, skills, training needs and age profiles, and cost them.

Consider the following issues:

- recruitment difficulties
- skills shortages
- high turnover
- staff retention problems
- professional aspirations and jealousies
- local economic and labour market analysis
- new professional regulations
- current trends across the local health economy, e.g. the creation of PCTs and strategic health authorities.

The next steps

- Use a phased approach to delivering changes.
- Think about what additional staff are needed.
- Consider any financial implications.
- Put in targets and milestones.
- Allow a lead-in time to develop new education models.

Review the process – as always, review on an annual basis and update where necessary.

Skill mix review

○ What are your plans to overcome any immediate recruitment or retention difficulties?

Some possible conclusions

- Upgrade roles and pay to a small number of more highly skilled staff.
- Downgrade roles and pay to a larger number of less skilled staff.
- Triage.

Practice manager role

The practice manager's role has changed considerably over the years and now the NHS is demanding very highly developed management skills. Not all practices have these skills in-house so some are appointing from outside. The most frequently occurring problem in general practice is that doctors often underestimate the level of management skill required. It is not unusual to find managers appointed from within who have very good organisational and interpersonal skills but no experience of business planning or organisational analysis and strategy. Practice managers need to have excellent interpersonal skills, a good level of self-awareness and an ability to research and analyse.

Practice managers need to be much more actively involved in strategic and clinical management. Rarely are managers involved in planning, monitoring and advising the partnership on clinical governance, systems management, alternative clinical management paths and business development. More often than not they are found covering in reception or typing upstairs for the doctors! For the profession and their businesses to develop:

 Managers need to develop and deliver strategically and manage the GPs, assisting them with their decision making process and manage, not administrate.

 Managers should be appointed to manage staff, and only in the most extreme circumstances should staff management issues be put on the agenda of a partnership meeting.

Practice managers have an uneasy task. However well they manage and however good communications and staff relationships appear, there will always be chaotic pockets and complaints of favouritism and poor delegation. Most practice managers confidently and ably fulfil an operational management role, are able to confront tough situations and demonstrate an ability to manage change and crisis. Most are comfortable with chairing and minuting meetings and are confident line managers. However, the most common problem is where managers are not managing strategically.

The practice manager of the future will need to be able to:

- develop leadership
- drive radical change
- re-shape culture
- exploit the organisation
- keep a competitive edge
- achieve constant renewal
- manage the motivators
- make team work work
- achieve Total Management Quality.[1]

What is the role of a manager?

The manager has a variety of roles within an organisation:

- commericial – buying and selling
- financial – obtaining capital and making optimal use of funds
- security
- accounting – stocktaking, balancing accounts, costing and analysis
- administration
- managerial:
  - planning
  - problem solving
  - decision making
  - networking

- co-ordinating
- organising
- supervising
- commanding
- controlling
- motivating
- measuring
- communicating
- managing conflict
- developing staff
- disciplining.

For all this s/he needs to have:

- technical competence
- social and human skills
- conceptual ability.

Here are some of the skills needed by practice managers specifically.

Recommended skills

- Education to degree level.
- Substantial experience in health, or awareness of health politics.
- Assertiveness and confidence.
- Excellent verbal and non-verbal communication skills.
- Financial acumen, numeracy and literacy.
- Good interpersonal skills.
- Computer literacy.
- Leadership skills and ability to motivate staff.
- Ability to team manage and understand team management.
- Prior knowledge and familiarity with NHS policy and culture.
- Ability to act responsibly, working within the limits of her own qualification, within known legal and professional boundaries and to be accountable for her own actions.
- Ability to act with integrity, and work honestly and conscientiously, respecting the boundaries of confidentiality.
- Ability to act in a caring and efficient way, respecting others' needs and individuality.
- Ability to listen well.
- Ability to retain her own professional and personal boundaries, treating colleagues and fellow professionals respectfully and with awareness and integrity.
- Awareness of her own ongoing need for professional and personal development.

- Ability to use own initiative.
- Ability to exercise discipline and control.

Practice management key tasks

- To understand, support and maintain the practice ethos.
- To represent the practice to all professional and public bodies.
- To facilitate consensus between partners, enabling decisions and ensuring they are acted on.
- To support the interests of all groups within the practice.
- To communicate effectively through writing, reading and presentation.
- To be responsible for day to day decisions.
- Meetings: preparing, chairing and achieving results.
- Consultation: using internal and external resources.
- Negotiation: formal and internal bargaining.
- Developing people: selection, planning succession, training and developing staff, appraisal, counselling, promotion and managing conflict.
- Managing teams: understanding psychology, motivation and organisational culture.
- Managing change.
- People management: dealing with stress, planning and using time and investing in and supporting staff.
- Taking control: managing the bosses, managing problems and decision making.
- To co-ordinate, implement and monitor within the practice.

Business management

- Strategic management: planning and analysing all aspects of the business and recommending options to partnership.
- Financial management: cash flow forecasting, managing debt, partnership tax, simple bookkeeping (practice accounts up to trial balance level), budgetary controls, costs and pricing, and long term planning.
- New technology: IT and presentation skills, knowledge of spreadsheets and data analysis packages and experience of using IT for audit and research.
- Estates and premises management.
- Product management: stock control, production control and measuring systems.
- Selling and marketing: customer relations, prospecting and promoting the business.

It is not always necessary for practices to appoint a full time manager. More and more practices are opting to employ a 'super manager' for specific project work, to augment the present management structure.

For further thoughts on the pros and cons of this, *see* the website.

Before appointing, it is essential the partnership agree and specify the practice manager's role, boundaries, expectations and responsibilities.

For the whole team

Mark off where your present manager meets the above criteria. Look honestly at the gaps and use this to point you in the right direction for training and development. Note the advantages and disadvantages, strengths and weaknesses of your own manager.

Staff management

The key function of staff management is to enable management to enhance the contributions people make to the success of an organisation. The range and scope of personnel activities are very wide.

For the whole team

Write down what you consider to be the functions of personnel management.

Compare your answer with the following list.

- Human resource planning and employment.
- Payroll administration including related rewards e.g. holiday and maternity pay.
- Organisational design.
- Management of work patterns.
- Observing current and future employment legislation and legal requirements.
- Training and development.
- Staff relations, services, welfare and safety.

Managing staff is not simply about ensuring disciplinary procedures are in place. Managers should fully understand the complexities of their organisation and have in place strategies for managing the risks of their staff failing to perform. Managers need to consider the ways staff are managed within their organisation.

When designing policies (staff charters, pay and reward strategies) certain factors need to be considered. What motivates people at work? How does the organisation communicate? What are the biggest influences in the organisation? What stops people performing at their best? What causes people the most stress? In this chapter, we look at the essential procedures – job descriptions and employment contracts – that you would expect all practices to have in place. However, all these essential contracts take into account an underlying belief in the need for people to have working rights.

⇒ **For the whole team**

What do you consider the rights of people at work are?

Some working rights

- A recognition and respect for people's needs and expectations at work.
- Full observance of all legal matters relating to employment.
- Just treatment.
- Fair reward for work done.
- Job security.
- Opportunities for training and development.
- Opportunities for career development.
- Good and safe working environment.

Is your organisation aware of (and does it respect) these rights? Or are you aware of them, but only pay lip service to them? Look for discrepancies and note them as items for change in your business plan.

Staff planning

> ⟹ **For the partners and manager**

Does the practice manager:

- ○ analyse existing staff resources by keeping a staff inventory
- ○ consider the impact of losses to and changes/developments in the staff
- ○ forecast the future needs of and demands on the practice
- ○ regularly reconcile supply and demand of staff?

Failures in communication cause the biggest problems in general practice, and the most stress for staff and management. Ensure your staff are clear about their role and give them the boundaries to function within by ensuring all policies and procedures are up to date.

Most practices recognise that staff are their most valuable asset and their greatest expense. Check that your practice is fulfilling its first line personnel management functions with:

- job descriptions
- contracts of employment
- disciplinary procedures
- grievance procedures
- annual appraisals
- training and development policies
- additional services, e.g. pensions, occupational health or counselling schemes for both staff and partners.

Check which need upgrading or amending. Use the above material to give an outline of any noticeable management problems.

Most practices coach and mentor staff as a way of developing. They appraise performance and counsel staff as a first line management approach for poor performance. Most have a complaints policy and patient charter. It is rarer to find audits and reports on complaints and appraisals through customer panels and customer surveys.

It is still common to find essential written contracts, policies and procedures are not in place, such as:

- confidentiality policy
- disciplinary procedures
- appraisal systems.

Write a paragraph about the practice manager's role in your business plan. *See* the website for example text.

Recruitment and selection

 **For the manager**

How does your practice demonstrate sound selection procedures?

The purpose of a selection procedure is to choose a person with the qualifications, skills, experience and personal attributes that would allow him/her to perform a pre-determined role. Does your practice consider the following for every job:

- ○ personnel planning
- ○ compliance with legal requirements and recommended codes of practice
- ○ job analysis
- ○ job description?

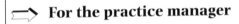 **For the practice manager**

Assumptions

- ○ Do you consider the selection of new members of staff to be a crucial decision?

○ Does the practice see that the consequences of a good or bad appointment remain within the practice for the duration of the staff member's employment?

○ Do you ensure that the staff selection procedures are fair, consistent and effective?

○ Do you see the selection process as an important public relations vehicle?

There is no right way other than that which is effective, legal and in conformity with the above.

If practices recruit, select and induct staff well, they avoid:

- absenteeism
- poor timekeeping
- staff turnover
- errors in work
- accidents
- breakages
- illness
- complaints
- discipline/grievance procedures
- dismissals.

For recruitment and selection templates, *see* the website. You need to consider:

- is there a job to be done?
- can it be filled?
- who might do the job?
- the job specification
- the candidate profile – this determines the person specification and personal competencies required
- the advert
- application screening
- references
- the job description
- the interview procedure
- decision making.

Reference

1   Heller R (1997) *In Search of European Excellence*. HarperCollins Business, Harlow.

CHAPTER 12

Policies and procedures

Induction

What were you told about in the first week of your current job?

What do you wish you had been told?

Does the practice have an induction procedure or pack? If so, who is it targeted at – ancillary staff, the clinical staff or the locum?

The first few weeks of any new job are very stressful. There is so much to learn: new faces, locations and procedures. It is the manager's job to ensure that new members of staff learn their own role, and that of the other members of staff, as quickly and smoothly as possible, in order that they may get on with what they are being paid to do as soon as possible.

The benefits of a planned induction

Employee benefits

- Avoids misunderstanding due to lack of basic knowledge.
- Helps employee fit in with established colleagues.
- Clarifies relationships with supervisors and/or subordinate staff.
- Increases job satisfaction.

Employer benefits

- Forms the basis of the job training to follow.
- Gets the new employee working productively in the shortest possible time.
- Shorter overall periods of training.
- Reduces staff turnover.
- Improved employer image because of employee's feeling of being valued.
- Creates a sense of purpose, responsibility and reliability among new staff.
- Creates and maintains a high standard of morale.
- Reduces the possibilities of disputes, misunderstandings, complaints and dismissals.
- Enhances the reputation of the practice.

A good induction takes time, and it is important not to underestimate this. Time spent explaining tasks is time well spent: a hasty induction leaves the new employee rushed, stressed and confused – not a good start to a hopefully long and fruitful working relationship. A quick induction also leaves the employee feeling as though they are not worth spending time on and all staff are entitled to feel individual and special. Research has shown that time spent on making staff feel personally cared for improves both the quality and quantity of their work – money is a less important factor.

Each practice will run differently; this is not important, but what is important is that the new employee is aware of the professional 'climate' at the practice, i.e. what is common practice. At induction, information is given that details some of the expected ways of working and forms part of the contract of employment. It certainly helps to avoid later possible disputes, and acts as a form of reference for new staff who may otherwise be confused about some of the things expected of them. An induction period also allows people who have never worked before more time to adjust to the work situation.

 For the manager

See the website for some good practice guidelines for inducting staff.

A good induction may be lengthy and time consuming to prepare, but the long term results are well worth the time spent. The aim is to have a team of relaxed, happy staff who feel well informed and clearly understand their role at work. In the long term you, as the employer, will benefit (as will the patients), as the practice should run more smoothly, efficiently and effectively. An induction procedure is part of good risk management; communication is improved and complaints minimised.

Ensuring confidentiality when the patient is a member of staff

Another area where practices make themselves vulnerable is when they allow, or encourage, staff members to register with the practice. If this cannot be avoided, then practices need to ensure they follow some safe procedural guidelines such as:

- giving the patient the opportunity to register with another practice if a medical report is required
- keeping any such staff records separately, under lock and key
- limiting the number of people who handle staff records to nominated staff or GPs only
- limiting access to computer records or keeping only manual records
- fostering a culture of confidentiality.

Appraisals

'A new performance Framework for Human Resources will be published ... all NHS employees will be assessed against performance targets and a new Improving Working Lives (IWL) standard. By April 2003 all NHS employers are expected to be accredited as putting the IWL into practice.'

The NHS Plan[1]

This will, without a doubt, include assessing and accrediting practices to ensure they have a useful appraisal system for both clinical and ancillary staff. Many managers do not like appraising staff and look for ways to avoid it. The main factor is usually time.

⇨ **For the manager**

What do you see as the advantages and disadvantages of appraisal systems?

Advantages

Disadvantages

Do you:

o hold annual performance appraisals for all staff (and if so, what type of appraisals are they and who does them)
o regularly identify training needs at appraisals
o use appraisals to set objectives and monitor progress
o use 360 degree (upward, downward and peer) appraisal
o have an appraisal system in place already for doctors
o feel you have time to appraise staff
o see the benefits of appraisal
o avoid giving constructive criticism
o give staff the space to self-appraise and assess their own strengths and weaknesses?

The appraisal interview

People achieve more when they are given adequate feedback on how they are performing, clear attainable goals and involvement in task setting. Appraisals are another way of demonstrating you believe in your staff. There is the opportunity for the manager to hear staff identify points they wish to work on; it then becomes easier for the manager to offer pointers of her own.

What is an appraisal?

- A formal system for looking at and building on the staff's strengths and minimising their weaknesses.
- An opportunity to look at jobs and job performance in a more structured way.
- A space for staff to self-assess their own needs and areas of difficulty.
- An opportunity to discuss potential for development.
- An opportunity to discuss training needs.[2]

Appraisals:

- usually occur annually
- can occur for new members of staff when the employee has been in post for about three to six months
- can highlight problems
- can assist succession planning
- can provide a manager with planning information
- can improve communications
- can determine suitability for career progression
- are related to organisational objectives
- have the support and commitment of the doctors
- have an established appeals procedure
- are subjective.

Appraisal is not:

- telling staff what is going wrong
- a disciplinary interview
- applied on the basis of insufficient, inadequate or irrelevant information
- ever dishonest
- presented as fact instead of opinion
- an opportunity to re-emphasise past problems.

⟹ **For the whole team**

Does the manager or supervisor:

- monitor staff performance
- make informal judgements on behaviour and work performance on a daily basis
- note positive as well as negative aspects of performance
- have the attitude that most people are well aware of their good and bad points, and will strive within a job to improve themselves
- respond appropriately and instantly to unacceptable behaviours, e.g. a complaint from a patient (these need disciplinary action and cannot be left until an annual appraisal is conducted)
- set standards for the staff
- make clear what is expected in terms of behaviour
- have written examples of what occurs if the staff contract has been breached?

Attitudes to colleagues and patients are transparent to the alert manager who spends time informally observing. Work well done needs to be praised too: thanks (verbal or written) are important if staff are expected to continue producing work of a high standard.

The annual appraisal is designed to look at the less obvious aspects of work performance: it gives an overall impression of your staff and helps both of you look at ways of extending and improving work performance. Most practices are run like a family business – even in large practices there are rarely more than a dozen or so ancillary staff employed. It is still important though to distribute appraisal preparation forms, or inform staff in advance that you will be interviewing, to give them time to prepare.

Ask the appraisee to consider the following points:

- their performance over the last 12 months, especially any problem areas or areas of achievement
- any training or help required in the job
- future ambitions.

Whoever does the interview needs to study the job description and see if any targets have been set after the last appraisal. If so, check and note results. Allow ample and uninterrupted time.

Follow up

Complete an appraisal form that looks at current problems and target areas for action. Give a copy to the member of staff.

Everyone appreciates it when their good work is noticed, and time spent on a good staff appraisal system is time well spent. Praise leads to constructive self-analysis which benefits the employer too. In practices where there are formal appraisal systems in use there tends to be less staff turnover and a happier working environment, which of course presents the practice to the outside world in a better light.

The disciplinary interview

 Too many practices avoid instigating disciplinary procedures.

Every practice has staff that overstep the mark, and there comes a time when it becomes necessary to intervene. It is then common to find practices who avoid using the correct disciplinary procedures. Giving criticism is never easy, and if given badly it can lead to avoidable and expensive resignation. However, if one member of staff behaves badly or consistently makes mistakes and is not disciplined, the lack of boundaries and clarity can create a feeling of uncertainty amongst the other members of staff. They too then may work in an undisciplined way as they see you condoning bad behaviour without sanction.

Does your practice have a formal disciplinary procedure? Effective managers:

- create clear guidelines, limits and boundaries
- are consistent and fair in their approach
- set guidelines at the beginning
- demonstrate that they understand the culture
- model mutual respect and clarity
- identify acceptable and unacceptable behaviour.

People need to know how far they can go and when they have crossed the limit. This is why it is essential to have a written job description and contract, so that staff will be aware when they have made a mistake and when their work is not up to standard (there is no argument, as they have seen and agreed the job description). It is then much easier to say 'As you are aware, this is what we expected of you and you have broken your side of the deal.'

The objective of the disciplinary interview is to correct mistakes or bad behaviour by helping the person to improve, thus preventing the situation from arising again. Staff should be aware of any systems for discipline in use. Most commonly a three tier system of verbal and written warnings is used: a mild misdemeanour will lead to a verbal warning; a more severe one a written warning (a note on the staff file which will be removed after an agreed time has lapsed); or dismissal if a complete breach of contractual terms occurs.

More often than not the first two warnings are used, and the last only as a final desperate measure. Occasionally it may be necessary to move through all three (when a stated behaviour does not improve, for example). It is worth noting that in a healthy practice, where staff feel happy and comfortable in your employ, they will volunteer to inform you of the occurrence before you are aware of it, as they trust you to support and help them.

 For the manager

Managers prepare! There are clearly good and bad ways to conduct these interviews. Look on the website for a review of some of the procedural guidelines.

References

1   Department of Health (2000) *The NHS Plan*. DoH, London.
2   Phillips A (2002) *Communication and the Manager's Job*. Radcliffe Medical Press, Oxford.

CHAPTER 13

Employment law and equalities

'Sometimes we forget that patients have aspirations identical to the rest of us. These do not include isolation, sleeping on the street, or spending the rest of their lives in Broadmoor.'

Health Service Journal (1999)

We should be creating services that address the priorities of patients and the public alike. So that we can do this, we need to address our own prejudices and attitudes.

Is your practice vulnerable?

'Most public bodies are institutionally racist and they include even the National Health Service.'

McPherson[1]

'The pre-NHS medical service was an "an ad hoc system suffering from severe anachronism, parochialism, inertia, stagnation, duplication and waste".'

Dean and Rigge[2]

Most practices define themselves as an 'equal opportunities employer', but can you demonstrate that your practice:

○ truly provides equal opportunities for all
○ treats everyone they have contact with (patients, staff and representatives of external organisations) equally and fairly?

Culturally, the health service does not provide a good model for anti-discriminatory practice, and this increases its vulnerability to claims from

those alleging discrimination. The new Human Rights Act and the Employment Relations Act (both recently in force) have highlighted a need for the
NHS to be acutely aware of anti-discriminatory practice. These Acts look at
several aspects of increased protection for workers.

Any NHS worker who ignores current law or good practice is putting their
organisation at great risk. The government, with an eye on the litigation
league tables, is recognising the importance of promoting good practice
within the NHS, and has even set up an equality reward to encourage the NHS
to improve equality of provision and opportunity.[3]

Racial discrimination is not the only problem. What are your attitudes as a
practice?

⇨ **For the whole team**

Can you demonstrate that you do not discriminate against:

- women
- gay men/lesbians
- travellers
- the elderly
- disabled people
- working people
- religious/ethnic groups
- people with emotional/mental health problems
- social classes 4 and 5?

Can all these groups access the services they need or the employment
opportunities they deserve?

The law is constantly changing. It is not expected that NHS managers keep
abreast of regulatory detail. The new Human Rights Act, for example, intro-
duces completely new concepts to English law, making the situation uncertain
as well as complex, even for specialists. Thus it would be unwise to look solely
to the law. Being proactive and instigating good practice is essential. It is
possible to have a broad sweep awareness and to at least be familiar with some
of the wider concepts of anti-discriminatory practice and to incorporate these
into all NHS-held personnel policies and procedures.

The NHS needs not only to be aware: to effect change, recommendations
need to be owned and incorporated into practice. This will require many
people within practices to change long held beliefs and patterns of behaviour.
The NHS is a system that needs a massive cultural overhaul if it is to take its
place proudly as a patient-oriented service, responding intelligently and
sensitively to the clinical and personal needs of its patients.

Practices can no longer be complacent about external allegations of racism, classism and sexism. Institutional racism has been defined as 'the collective failure of an organisation to provide an appropriate and professional service to people because of their colour, culture or ethnic origin. It can be seen or detected in processes, attitudes and behaviour which amount to discrimination through unwitting prejudice, ignorance, thoughtlessness and stereotyping which disadvantage minority ethnic people.'[1] This definition could usefully broaden to incorporate all dimensions of discrimination against sexuality, class, disability or culture.

 For the whole team

Look at the following list and see where you fit. There are certain factors in our society which shift our sense of power in relation to others; some factors shift it up and some shift it down.[4]

Factors which shift power up	Factors which shift power down
being aged between 25 and 45	being working class
white	being black or from an ethnic minority
articulate	having a strong regional accent
educated or professional	not speaking English well or stammering
employed	being disabled in any way
a man	being short or 'ugly'
'attractive'	being a victim (of violence or abuse)
being rich	being 'different' in any way, through culture or sexuality
being 'average'	having an obvious mental health problem

Some questions

○ What are your feelings about the above?
○ What assumptions and attitudes do you already hold?
○ Why?
○ How might these attitudes impact on other individuals around you?
○ However you identify, think about the experience of your opposite number for a minute: what would it feel like to be more or less powerful?
○ How do you act and behave when faced with your prejudice? Are you dismissive, patronising, hurtful or scared?
○ Do you need to change?

Make a list of all the negative ways certain groups of people can be described through age, gender, sexuality and disability, e.g. 'old codger', 'bent' or 'spastic'.

○ Have you ever used a term that would upset or offend?

- o   Do you make assumptions about people, for example, assume everyone is heterosexual?
- o   Have you ever been challenged about your use of language?
- o   Have you ever responded to a patient in a way that may have deterred or inhibited them from using your services?

Have you ever examined some of your beliefs and prejudices about your colleagues? We tend to act tribally, we feel safer in groups, and one way we reinforce this feeling of safety is to poke fun at the 'other'.

Look at the following remarks, and see if you can work out who they are describing: the managers, doctors or patients. What do these remarks tell us about our beliefs?

- •   These people are very frustrating to the other tribes because they don't always do what they are told or what is good for them. They often like drinking and smoking and eating food with salt in it.
- •   Their language is made up of diseases and populations.
- •   Most of them live in places called *institutions*, which allows them to protect themselves from where the patients live.
- •   They organise into groups for self-protection called families and friends.
- •   They have an interesting approach to relaxation which is to work even more at evenings and weekends and they are, therefore, a very intense and earnest tribe who often bore their partners and other tribes rigid.
- •   They form into groups for self-protection, which they call *Royal Colleges* and *Associations*.
- •   Their language is made up of systems, organisations and structures.
- •   Their thought process is interesting, and unlike the rest of the tribes they think in terms of analysis, decisions and visions (the visions often seem like hallucinations to the other tribes).
- •   They sometimes have difficulty communicating with the other tribes and use different and loud words, which causes particular concern during something called *consultations*.[5]

A quarter of us will, at some time in our lives, be disabled in some way – socially or medically. The NHS needs to keep aware of the barriers we place in front of those who are trying to access the services they are entitled to. Think about the barriers in your practice:

- •   environmental: outside (lack of transport, timetables and overcrowding); and inside (poor lighting, cluttered corridors, inadequate switches)
- •   institutional/organisational: complicated forms, policies for smooth running (e.g. calling at specified times and queue management)
- •   attitudinal.

Can you afford to continue putting up these barriers? This chapter addresses some of the reasons practices need to address the ways they work, and put right any wrongs.

⟹ **For the doctors and manager**

Checklist for practice health.

o   Do you fully understand the complexities and culture of your organisation?
o   Do you conform to all relevant employment law?
o   Does the practice anticipate the impact of new legislation?
o   Do you train on disability awareness and equal opportunities?
o   Do you coach and mentor staff?
o   Do you counsel staff as a first line management approach for poor performance?
o   Do you examine reports on complaints, consultation and referral rates?
o   Do you organise other investigative systems such as customer panels and customer surveys?

Practices need managers who can fully understand the complexities and culture of their organisation and have in place strategies for anticipating and managing the risks of their staff failing to perform. The practice needs to be proactive and anticipate the legislation. Organisations need to coach and mentor staff as a way of developing, and counsel staff as a first line management approach for poor performance. Instigate and develop self or peer appraisal systems for clinicians too, through examining reports on complaints, consultation and referral rates. Organise other investigative or appraisal systems such as customer panels and customer surveys.

Look at your areas of vulnerability. These can often be found in the interview process. Too many practices increase their vunerability by ignoring the Sex Discrimination Act 1975, for example by quizzing female staff at interview on their child bearing plans. What are the attitudes towards disability? Organisationally, negativity often prevails even if it is not publicly expressed. If this occurs, address it by planning some training and development work around attitude change.

Applying the culture

Discriminatory practice often occurs where there is a long held power imbalance. The NHS can no longer afford to practice in parochial and patriarchal ways. Managers need to take every opportunity to point out where discriminatory practice has occurred. Without such challenge the NHS continues to be at risk. At the moment, both doctors and managers tend to regard power inequalities as natural, necessary and beneficial. They attach little value to having a supportive superior and back a medical ascendancy model of management.

This prevailing culture prevents any real change.

Practices need to guard against a hierarchical and patriarchal management style where self-interest prevents any real change.

At present, a doctor's professional autonomy and attitudes are seldom questioned by those outside the medical profession and few doctors feel that financial or managerial decisions affect their professional practice in any way.[6] Attitudes can change, but the challenges have to be effective and not provocative. Political awareness can grow where workers demonstrate mutual respect for each other's differences. Change can only be effected when managers are given the authority to manage. Practice managers and doctors traditionally have an uneasy relationship – the manager's role can often be tokenistic, with no real power or autonomy. An important part of business planning is to ascertain if the manager's role is in name only.

 For the partners and manager

In medicine, 53% of those training to be doctors are women, with the percentage still restricted at entrance to medical school. Under the Human Rights Act, the right to equal treatment opens up the risk of employment claims from women who allege discrimination based on sexual discrimination at source. Practices have to be scrupulous in their dealings with female partners, and ensure that discrimination does not occur. Challenge gender, class and race imbalances. The entrenched cultural problems within the NHS are limiting.

Consider if your practice is vulnerable.

○ Do your female partners work part time?
○ Do they take on the brunt of the childcare commitments in their family?
○ Are they finding attitudes prevail that make it difficult to progress their careers?
○ Are the doctors developing ways of working in partnership with client groups?
○ Do your staff demonstrate hostility or reluctance in involving users in service developments or even their own treatments?
○ Are the services provided accessible to everyone?

The majority of NHS workers are committed to equality issues and their organisation. But to move they need to be honest about power sharing and their own resistance to losing that power. They need to recognise and understand oppression and difference and be aware of their cultural advantage. In most organisations, negative attitudes prevail around diversity and difference; often not publicly expressed, but frequently expressed internally. To address this, plan training and development work around attitude change.

Group methods are most effective as they encourage observation through reflection. Training should not just be about the current legislation, but about discrimination and raising awareness of oppressive practices, encouraging staff to become aware of their own prejudices and responses. The objective is to raise awareness with the aim of changing attitudes rather than to impose judgements – people will change once they understand.

For some further training ideas, *see* the website.

The legislation

> ⇒ **For the manager**

Part of staff management is being aware of current legislation and its application to general practice. In your business plan you will need to demonstrate awareness of, and the application of, Employment law, all relevant Contract law, Acts and Directives.

Employment law can be formulated by:

- statute law (acts of parliament)
- case law (tribunals)
- European Community Directives and court decisions
- common law.

Are you aware of the following Acts?

- Health and Safety at Work Act 1974
- Equal Pay Act 1970
- Rehabilitation of Offenders Act 1974
- Race Relations Act 1976
- Employment Rights Act 1993
- The Employment Relations Act 1999
- Sex Discrimination Act 1975 and 1986
- Health and Safety at Work Regulations 1992
- Human Rights Act 1998
- Disability Discrimination Act 1995
- The National Minimum Wage Act 1988
- The Public Interest Disclosure Act 1998
- Working Time Regulations 1998.

Are you aware of the following? (*See* the website for further details.)

- The Fairness at Work White Paper
- Family Friendly Policies

- The 1999 Employment Relations Act
- Maternity rights
- Working Time Directives.

 Recommended action to reduce vulnerability.

- Check you give all your employees all the job opportunities offered within your organisation.
- Allow all staff the opportunity to attend job reviews, disciplinary hearings and redundancy consultations, even if they are on sick or maternity leave.
- Carefully consider all requests from employees who wish to alter their work patterns. Demonstrate your thinking. You may need to prove it. Keep all the necessary paperwork on file, and document all your decision making. The files may be used if an employee sues the practice.

Data Protection Act 1984 and 1998

The 1984 Act gave individuals extensive rights to examine personal information held on computers – the new Act strengthens this right by extending the right of access to manual records. The legislation hopes to restrict the extent to which people are discriminated against in the workplace. Practice managers need to be aware of this when keeping notes: there is no room for recording anything that may be considered inflammatory: racist, ageist, sexist or homophobic comments would not be tolerated. Employees will be able to ask employers to delete information that is unwarranted or causes distress or damage. If employers find it difficult to justify comments that are irrelevant to job performance, these comments must be removed.

The legislation is complex and some measures may not be in place until as late as 2007. Employees will be able to see previous but not current records and references, until they arrive at a new job. If requested, the data needs to be produced within 30 days. Employers have good reason to consider introducing a more equal opportunities approach if they have not already done so – multiple choice assessments for instance would obviate the need to make additional or explanatory notes. See this as an opportunity to be more open in your hiring and firing procedures, and try and resist 'going underground' by limiting your record writing or writing in code.

Health and Safety

The TUC are calling for effective workplace policies that ensure employees are supported, not punished. It is deemed good practice for organisations to develop constructive healthy workplace policies that address any illness or emotional problem that has stigma attached, and provide supportive, not punitive, assistance to their employees.

All employers have a duty of care to their staff under their Health and Safety at Work Act 1974. Further regulations (management of Health and Safety Regulations 1992) require 'health surveillance' which involves detailed risk assessment for employees.

 Practice managers must take active steps to ensure they are protecting their staff from, and managing the risks of, the impacts of stress at work.

 Managers be aware!

- Stress affects some 60% of the population at any one point.
- It is an implied term of every contract that employers will take reasonable care of their employee's safety and well-being, and this includes mental as well as physical health.
- Employers are legally bound to provide a safe system of work and are required to make regular assessments of potential risk to likely ill-health.

Good employers move beyond fulfilling their legislative responsibilities towards interpreting the legislation. This lessens the organisation's vulnerability to being sued under the various employment legislation banners. Small businesses, such as general practice, are particularly vulnerable.

 For the managers

Are you taking active steps in your organisation? Are you protecting your staff from:

- bullying and harassment
- excessive workload
- the impact of new technology
- uncertainty and change
- short term contracts
- crisis and trauma?[6]

The practice needs to demonstrate how far they are managing these risks.

- Do you provide in-house counselling services for staff who are struggling?
- Do you have a people management policy which demonstrates significant concern for employee welfare?
- Are strategies written with staff and not top driven?

It is good risk management, particularly in the light of the recent equalities legislation, to ensure the organisation cannot be accused of discriminatory practice. Include a section on each of the relevant policies or Acts within your business plan, and describe how far the practice complies.

Example

The practice is aware of the Health and Safety at Work Act (HASAWA) 1974, and carries out systematic assessments of workplace risks, including 'near misses', and records any significant findings.

Note if the practice abides by good practice guidelines and is aware of other important legislation:

- Equal Pay Act 1970
- Race Relations Act 1976
- Contract law
- ACAS codes of conduct.

Applying the principles

Record keeping

Checklist for employers

- Clarify the purpose of all interviews.
- Be aware of the Good Practice Guidelines: confidentiality, access and equality.
- Be aware of the relevant legislation.
- Keep in mind the need to act reasonably within the law.
- Select, promote and treat all individuals on the basis of their relevant merits and abilities.
- As an employer you need to demonstrate you are only interested in your employees' current and future ability to do the job you are employing them for.
- Keep personal prejudices to yourself: the law is only interested in justified opinions.
- Standardise your record keeping system.
- Use a fair and equal system for evaluating the results.

For the manager

Can the practice apply the above principles? Are all the practice procedures fair, consistent, effective and legal? Be honest! Remember the purpose of the business plan is to highlight problems as well as good practice.

For examples of good interviewing practice, *see* the website.

 Good preparation is the key to handling any interview.

Consider how you would prepare questions for the following interview types, and how your questions would differ:

- the selection interview
- the medical interview
- the counselling interview.

Recommendations for good practice

 Your organisation is vulnerable if you do not take note of these recommendations.

- Coach and mentor key staff as a way of developing them; appraise performance and counsel staff as a first line management approach for poor performance.
- Introduce 360 degree appraisal so all staff in the organisation self and peer appraise.
- Audit and report on complaints and appraise through customer panels and customer surveys.
- Be aware of your own attitudes.
- Never tolerate oppressive humour or comments in your organisation. Build in such a clause in your patients' charter and staff contract. There is no place for oppression in the NHS.
- Use literature to enlighten not confuse. Write to inform not impress. Write posters and leaflets plainly and clearly, and make them available in different languages. Use your interpreting services.
- Involve and empower patients. Talk with, not at patients. Consult rather than inform. Ask not tell. Listen more, and impose less.
- Consider if the services you provide (to your patients or staff) are provided impartially to all people, irrespective of their gender, ability and background, or their sexual, cultural, social and personal orientation. If not, change.

- Staff managers must avoid the easy way out – is there a tendency to inappropriate permissiveness, where bad performance is ignored or not dealt with?
- Measure and set targets for staff absence and turnover rates.
- Always seek legal advice if in doubt.
- Check your recruitment and retention policies.
- Devise anti-discriminatory training programmes for the entire organisation.
- Draft new policies dealing with parental leave and time off for urgent domestic incidents.
- Ensure early stage involvement of personnel in disciplinary or grievance issues.

 For the manager

- Do you use a quantitative, not qualitative assessment procedure in interviewing? It is never appropriate for an organisation to make inquiries regarding the assumed status of individuals.
- Do you have effective workplace policies to ensure employees are supported, not punished? It is good practice to develop constructive healthy workplace policies. Support and assistance must be offered to any illness, emotional problem or disability that has stigma attached.
- Have you introduced an equal opportunities approach in interviews? Multiple choice assessments obviate the need to make additional or explanatory notes.
- Are you open in your hiring and firing procedures? Do you resist 'going underground' by limiting your record writing or writing in code?
- Have you got an appraisal system for doctors and staff? Consider introducing a 360 degree appraisal so all staff in the organisation self and peer appraise.
- Do you tolerate oppressive humour or comments in your organisation? Stamp on this now. Build in such a clause in your patients' charter and staff contract. There is no place for oppression in the NHS.
- Do you use literature to enlighten not confuse? Write to inform not impress. Write posters and leaflets plainly and clearly, and make them available in different languages. Use your interpreting services.
- Do you involve and empower patients? Describe how. Talk with, not at patients. Consult rather than inform. Ask, don't tell. Listen more, and impose less.
- Consider if the services provided (to your patients or staff) are really provided impartially to all people, irrespective of their gender, ability and background, or their sexual, cultural, social and personal orientation. If not, change.

○   Do your staff managers take the easy way out – is there a tendency to inappropriate permissiveness, where bad performance is ignored or not dealt with? Change this. Be in charge.

○   Do you measure and set targets for staff absence and turnover rates?

○   Have you drafted new policies dealing with parental leave and time off for urgent domestic incidents?

○   Have you extended your employment rights to bank staff, locum and casual workers? This is now required by law.

○   Have you instigated additional self or peer appraisal systems for clinicians through regularly auditing complaints, consultation and referral rates? Do you sign up to PDPs?

○   Healthy organisations are strongly influenced by humanistic psychology, where openness, trust and belief in individual growth are paramount. Build an organisational framework that is humanitarian, where the management style is open, reflective, listening and interested.

○   Look at your areas of vulnerability. These can often be found in the interview process. What are the attitudes towards disability, age, sexuality? Organisationally, negativity often prevails even if it is not publicly expressed. If this occurs, con-sider attitude training through group work; encouraging observation through reflection.

○   Look at who you employ in your organisation – does the mix reflect your local community? When you advertise jobs, consider advertising in selected newspapers or periodicals to encourage minority groups to apply, e.g. the Pink Paper for lesbians and gay men, the black or Asian press.

○   Ask or survey staff for their ideas on change.

○   Make certain recruitment and selection are visibly fair; sexist comments must not be tolerated.

○   Regularly update disciplinary and grievance procedures, reminding both staff and employees of their responsibilities.

○   Identify any future organisational training needs through appraisal; cost up training requests through appraisals. Do not ignore the outcome of appraisal through lack of resources, but redesign jobs to increase motivation if necessary.

○   Actively survey the number of disadvantaged groups or minorities in your organisation; be aware of their existence, how vulnerable they are to discriminatory comments, bullying and harassment, and act constructively if this occurs.

○   If setting up quality groups, review their performances formally – perhaps through anonymous questionnaire.

○   Suggest instigating a cafeteria system within the pay policy: offer a selection of entitlements so that staff select the one that matches their needs best, e.g. pension scheme, extra holiday entitlement or childcare allowances.

- ○ Avoid writing notes on staff that are judgmental or potentially discriminating.
- ○ Do you have an anti-bullying and anti-harassment culture?
- ○ Do you give your staff written guidance on what is considered unacceptable behaviour in the practice?
- ○ Do you have a whistleblowing policy?
- ○ Do you acknowledge that bullying and harassment are problems for the organisation? Be honest! Have you issued a clear statement saying that these behaviours will not be tolerated, including:
  - the steps you would take to prevent it
  - the responsibilities of line managers
  - confidentiality rules in the event of any complaint
  - timescales for action
  - investigation procedures
  - training
  - protection
  - how the policy will be implemented?
- ○ Do you as a manager or employer model good practice by not, for example:
  - spreading malicious rumours or insulting someone (particularly on gender, race, disability or sexuality grounds)
  - allowing exclusion or victimisation
  - allowing misuse of power or position
  - allowing unwelcome sexual advances – touching, standing too close or displaying offensive materials
  - making threats about job security without foundation
  - deliberately undermining colleagues by constant criticism or overloading them with work
  - intentionally blocking promotion or training opportunities?
- ○ Do you have an equal opportunities policy which:
  - aims to offer equity of access
  - applies to all staff and volunteers within the organisation
  - is intended to be used as a tool for continuous improvement
  - acknowledges that in society some groups or individuals are unwittingly, or wittingly, discriminated against
  - aims to eradicate all forms of such discrimination
  - outlines the necessary disciplinary and grievance procedures that would be followed
  - is applied to practice in all areas
  - applies to all procedures across the organisation
  - communicates with disadvantaged groups, removing barriers which may deter them from seeking a service
  - gives people from such groups the opportunity to be represented within the practice

- ensures services are delivered sensitively, recognising linguistic and cultural barriers
- ensures all staff are offered equal opportunities training regularly
- works within current legislation
- is reviewed annually?

In general practice, because primary care functions in the main as small, non-unionised organisations, employment claims are rare. As a consequence many oppressive practices are tolerated where they should not be. Managers in primary care in particular must understand that awareness of equality issues should go beyond admonishing a doctor for asking an interviewee about their family commitments. These issues need to be addressed urgently, so that the new anti-discriminatory NHS will function effectively, listen well, and address the communities it serves.

For more information, *see* the website.

References

1   McPherson W, Sir (1999) In: *The Independent*. 25 February.

2   Dean M and Rigge M (1998) In: *The Guardian*. 1 July.

3   NHS Equality Awards www.doh.gov.uk/nhsequality

4   Cruse Bereavement Care (2000) *Making It Happen: working towards equality*. Cruse, London.

5   Griffiths P (1996) *Beyond Management*. Institute of Health Service Management, London.

6   May A (1998) Streets ahead on quality. *Health Service Journal*. **10 December**.

Further information

- ACAS Reader Ltd provides the following titles:
  - *Employing People: a handbook for small firms*
  - *Holidays and Holiday Pay*

  Tel: 01455 852225

  www.acas.org.uk
- Croner's *Legislation Tracker* for the most significant pieces of recent and forthcoming UK and European employment legislation www.croner.co.uk
- *Data Protection Register* is available from ODPR:

  Tel: 01625 545737
- The Health and Safety Executive provides a range of titles

  HSE Infoline: 0870 154 2200

  www.hse.gov.uk

- The Inland Revenue provides the following titles:
  - *Employing Staff: a guide to regulatory requirements*
  - *Financing Your Business*
  - *A Guide to Help for Small Businesses*
  - *A Guide to Starting in Business*
  Tel: 0845 7646 646
- The Maternity Alliance publishes *Pregnant at Work*, available from:
  The Maternity Alliance
  45 Beech Street
  London EC2P 2LX
- Anti-discriminatory training manual from:
  Cruse House
  126 Sheen Road
  Richmond
  Surrey TW9 1UR
  Tel: 020 8939 9530
  www.crusebereavementcare.org.uk

CHAPTER 14

Personnel v human resource management

'In real life the most practical advice for leaders is not to treat pawns like pawns, nor princes like princes, but all persons like persons.'

JM Burns

According to the NHS Plan, NHS staff want:

- more staff
- fair pay
- more training
- improved management skills
- joined up working
- less bureaucracy
- better working conditions
- aids to recruitment and retention
- flexible working patterns.[1]

The government has outlined some of the ways they want to improve the working lives of NHS staff. They are intensifying and encouraging training, with more – and more accessible – courses, encouragement of flexible working practices and mentoring of returning staff. They are stating that 'the way NHS employers treat staff will be part of the core performance measures and linked to the financial resources they receive.' To make this possible they are developing:

- a new Performance Framework for Human Resources
- new Improving Working Lives (IWL) standards
- an occupational health service for all doctors and staff
- employee accreditation standards. By April 2003 all NHS employers are expected to be accredited as putting IWL standards into practice.

In this chapter we look at some of the ways we can improve relationships in practices by examining leadership, communication, personality and motivation.

IWL standards

> ➩ **For the whole team**

Can your organisation prove it is not just applying the principles of the legislation but:

- investing in the training and development of staff
- tackling discrimination and harassment
- improving diversity
- applying a zero tolerance policy to violence against staff
- reducing workplace accidents
- providing better occupational health and counselling services
- conducting annual attitude surveys
- asking staff relevant questions and acting on the key messages
- providing access to learning for all NHS staff without a professional qualification
- committed to providing flexible working conditions
- involving staff in the design and development of better working practices?

Some of this now sounds familiar, but how does a practice put in place mechanisms to assist these new working practices? There needs to be a transitional stage, to shift the practice culture to a place where it can deal with some of the above issues.

In general practice, personnel issues are usually managed reasonably well, where management deals with the short term, operational level of business management. Human resource management, however, is strategic and long term. This aspect of work is often left uncontrolled.

In the last chapter we dealt with some of the legal and ethical issues to consider in practice management. We saw how practices need to develop people management policies which demonstrate significant concern for employee welfare. We noted how it is good risk management, particularly in the light of recent equalities legislation, to ensure the organisation cannot be accused of discriminatory practice. Clinical governance will be a challenge for organisations and staff. Practices who invest in their staff by ensuring the following will be the gainers:

- staff are well trained and competent
- there is a good skill mix within the practice

- the working environment is safe and comfortable
- working practices are cost effective.

We now look beyond people management, policies and laws, to whole system management. If managers work on cultural issues, the organisation will move beyond directing and controlling people. People management then becomes a key element in the strategic planning of a business.

One of the problems with general practice is that it is a small business. Celia Brayfield[2] noted that firms of less than 25 people are especially prone to:

- dodgy business practices
- not adopting modern management methods easily
- having a problem investing in people
- often escaping welfare obligations
- reluctancy to budget for the effects of illness or maternity leave
- unstable employment
- difficulties adapting to change.

Is this true of your practice?

One of the ways you can measure the happiness and health of your organisation is to look at some of the key issues involved in staff satisfaction:

- good communication
- democratic leadership
- leaders promote innovation
- staff consultation
- training and development needs met
- team or group working
- meeting motivational needs
- understanding culture.

All these issues need to be addressed in your practice analysis.

Leadership

Practices can only achieve by the co-ordinated efforts of their members, and it is the manager's task to get work done through other people. Managers, however, are only effective if they adopt an appropriate style of behaviour. Thus the manager must understand the nature of leadership.

Here are some thoughts on leadership:

- leaders are born not made
- leadership skills can be learned and developed
- leadership transforms the performance of the organisation
- leadership style has an effect on those led
- there is no single style of leadership appropriate to all situations.

Where leadership is top driven: command and control are the key words, and the power base is determined by the owner or managers.[3] Now that the primary care brief is widening it is becoming more common to find people working in a situation where the power base is held by expert teams, not individuals; people who work collectively on clearly defined subject areas. This is a more modern and popular way of working.

Of course, working within a clearly defined autocratic, hierarchical and bureaucratic organisation has its benefits. Staff know where they sit, their responsibilities are clearly defined and change is easy to impose. However, it is not a modern or popular way of working, rarely uses all the skills within the organisation, and is not good for staff morale. Younger staff in particular now demand and expect to work more flexibly, and have their ideas, wishes and responses listened to and acted on more tolerably. Hierarchical working also breeds discriminatory practice as it only incorporates a one-sided idea (the bosses') of correctness, standards and principles.

A more positive system befits organisations hoping to promote a more innovative environment. One that encourages creativity and demonstrates respect for its employees.

⇒ **For the whole team**

Different styles of leadership are appropriate for different stages of a business.[4]

Where is your business now and have you got the managerial skills required to meet its needs?

Where is your business?	Person needed	Skills needed
A new venture?	Champion	Team driving. To provide wide range of management skills. To have innovation and energy.
Entering growth stage	Tank commander	Manager to develop strong, supportive team. Driving leadership qualities.
Mature. Meeting boundaries erected by competitors	Housekeeper	To ensure efficiency and economy. Planning skills. Cost control. Sound personnel policies.
Very mature. Premature decline	Lemon squeezer	To extract maximum benefit. Tough and innovative. Cut costs. Improve productivity. Reduce staffing levels.

In successful practices devolved responsibilities mean all the skills within the organisation are used fully, which is good for staff morale.

 For the whole team

Look critically at your practice.

○ Is your leadership style relaxed and accommodating?
○ Is leadership top driven?
○ Can you draw lines of command and control?
○ Is the power base determined by the owner/managers?
○ Do people work collectively?
○ Do staff understand their responsibilities?
○ Is change easy to impose?
○ Do people have their ideas, wishes and responses listened to and acted on?
○ Who defines standards and principles?
○ Do you promote innovation?
○ How do you demonstrate respect for your employees?

In most practices, managers who are strapped for time write the policies using information derived from published guides. These are usually circulated for consultation, read and amended by the partners, who may or may not actively consult staff. In general, this model results in policies being adhered to, but in some areas compliance is not good, and staff are unhappy. This way of managing demonstrates direction and control. The policies clearly determine the way staff may expect to be disciplined, the way they are expected to fit in with the organisational objectives. This approach is designed to make unilateral management action more palatable. Senior management decide the overall strategy and plan, and nobody else is involved.

Best practice shows us organisations where the decision making is devolved down, and ideas are fed up. The use of 'quality groups' demonstrates good employee involvement (as recommended in the 'excellence' literature).[5] Here a series of workplace groups are set up to initiate and develop workplace initiatives. Responsibility for creativity and ideas is devolved down, so everyone in the organisation has responsibility for being part of the decision making process. Change, initiative, and learning through trial and error are then not feared but viewed positively. People are encouraged by being involved and directing the agenda for change.

Practice managers need to lead their organisation towards the cutting edge of change. A healthy, modern employer would be able to demonstrate some of the models outlined in the 'excellence' literature. It is possible to shift from a simple, perhaps bureaucratic, structure to a more complex, mature organisational approach to human resource management.

Most general practices work hierarchically. Because of this, they need to guard against discriminatory practice, which incorporates a one-sided idea (the bosses') of correctness, standards and principles.

Staff are rarely consulted, and their ideas and input are not often used. Staff need to be trusted to get on with the job. Innovation should be encouraged as it encourages creativity and demonstrates respect for employees.

Does your organisation

- devolve decision making?
- feed up ideas?
- use 'quality groups'?
- encourage employee involvement?

Simplistic models of people management seek to direct and control, and see people as dispensable.

 In a lot of practices staff complain that their work is fragmented and staff would welcome more responsibility.

Reorganisation of workload could make more of this possible e.g. making one person responsible for an entire job from beginning to end (administering the immunisation and cervical cytology targets, for example). Such jobs need consolidating.

See the website for some other leadership considerations and patterns.

Communication

Tony Benn, in *The Independent* on 27 October 1996, noted one of the most common people management techniques used today when he said:

> *'Discussion is the most radical thing in the world, which is why no system ever wants you to talk about anything. They don't want you to get together and come to a conclusion because it may not be the kind of conclusion they like.'*

Team working

Group working assists practices to move towards a more mature organisational approach. Group and team working improves communication. By seeking opinions on the way things are organised, management ensures everyone agrees on the objectives and nature of the working relationship.

- How do people fit in to this organisation?
- What do they think and feel about working here?
- What are we getting right, and wrong?

Plans for change are fully discussed, demonstrating an objective to maximise the commitment of employees. Individuals are encouraged to develop the habits of self-discipline and initiative, and the organisation is seen as organic – always moving and changing. If some of these methods are adopted, the organisation will have something approaching a TQM approach.

Carlisle and Parker presented the following model of an integrated and effective organisation.[6] How far does your practice fit this vision?

- Managed through shared vision.
- Systems designed to liberate.
- Appropriate involvement and co-operation from employees.
- Customer led.
- Emphasis on quality.
- Focused on long term results.
- Biased to action.

Checklist for practice health

- Do you see people as dispensable?
- Do your doctors have a paternalistic management style where they seek the middle line: fair play, often unilaterally and without consultation with you?
- Do you work well in groups and teams?
- Does management ensure everything is discussed and everyone agrees?
- Is there any favouritism and manipulation?

In most practices, there is room for increased motivation by continuing to develop a devolved management style. There is more opportunity for encouraging an increase in personal responsibility and initiative and improving communication. Practices need to be much more open in their dealings with staff, and everyone needs to be discouraged from manipulative behaviour – seeking to gain favourites and seeking out individual opinions.

Survey the staff

We know that one way, indeed the best way, to find out how people see your surgery is to ask. Use the views collected from people in the practice to answer the following questions.

- Is the business culture relaxed and accommodating?
- Is the business culture fixed and bureaucratic?
- Is communication good?

- How are staff kept informed?
- Are their concerns acted on or ignored?
- Are everyone's views respected and acted on?

As we saw in the last chapter, a good equal opportunities employer would try to ensure a cultural and ethnic mix of employees that reflect the general population around them. There would be concern if all the employees were white and middle class in an area of the country with a significant black working class population. Can you demonstrate an anti-discriminatory ethos? Can you show how you have listened to all your staff and acted on their opinion?

Policies and procedures

As well as a patient's charter, the practice may wish to consider developing a staff charter that shows staff are both informed and consulted about matters likely to affect their employment. This would positively reflect the employer's views on fairness and equity in employment, and stand the organisation in good stead should an employee sue them for unfair dismissal/work-induced, stress-related illness etc.

Staff charter

Staff should have the right to:

- be informed and consulted about matters likely to affect their employment
- be treated fairly, with courtesy and understanding to ensure equity for all and respect for individual differences
- be fully and properly trained to do the job they are employed to do
- be rewarded fairly for the contribution they make to the organisation, taking into account effort, skill and achievement
- comment or complain to their employers without fear or prejudice
- be able to feed their ideas and views back to a management structure that will listen and act on them.

Meetings

Best practice shows us organisations where the decision making is devolved down, and ideas are fed up. Such practices make good use of meeting time, which demonstrates good employee involvement. Given that the biggest complaint in general practice is usually poor communication, practices that make good use of meeting time go a long way towards alleviating this.

Partnership meetings are not usually public events, but feedback to staff from these meetings is rare; at best haphazard and partial, at worst absent.

 Practices need to develop a mechanism to feed back to the staff following partnership meetings or external reviews. Staff need to feel included in the major decision making.

Here are some facts about meetings in general practice.

- Most GPs hate meetings.
- Most practice managers hate meetings.
- Most staff hate meetings.
- Meetings are essential to foster good two-way communication.

Make a note in your business plan about the number and type of meetings you have.

Note whether they are well chaired or not, are organised or not, have good attendance, are held frequently enough or whether there is an absence of agendas and minutes.

- How often are they held?
- Are they managed well?
- What are the problems?

Communication styles

Healthy organisations seem to be strongly influenced by an organisational framework that is humanitarian, building on ideas from Carl Rogers where the management style is open, reflective, listening and interested.[7]

For this to happen, be prepared to learn how to communicate well.

- Eighty five percent of communication is non-verbal, communicated in gestures, facial expression and tone of voice.
- Another way to communicate verbally is through writing (memos, reports etc.).
- We communicate in groups, in meetings and on the telephone.

Write down all the ways you communicate at work. Note down why you think there may be crossed wires in each situation.

- In any two-way communication both of you need to be interested and involved.
- Both sides need to be willing to be open and honest.
- Both sides need to feel heard and understood.
- The atmosphere needs to be comfortable.
- Even if the talking is difficult, the important things get said.
- Conversations have to make a difference. Something useful or satisfying happens as a result.

Make a note of the good and poor communicators in your practice.

Good communicator	Poor communicator
Understands everyone has a different inner world, and different motivations and experiences	Wants everyone to be like themselves, makes assumptions
Is open to whatever	Attacks or threatens
Is interested by difference	Patronises or puts down
Respects and values your views	Trivialises views
Displays clarity, stays on track	Rambles
Reflects back to show understanding, responds with interest	Always misses the point
Checks out it is a good time to talk	Barges in regardless
Gives people the opportunity to respond	Overloads or bores
Prompts	Takes up all the room
Asks	Tells

In summary, good communicators:

- read the situation
- engage attention
- make the meaning clear

- tell the story
- look for clues
- check understanding
- tell the truth
- summarise.

Personality

Personality differences can be a source of great strength and creativity or conflict. Managers need to be able to recognise potential and harness talent to meet the needs of the organisation. It is common to find that practices have their own personality; general practice is often run as a family business, with, in psychoanalytic terms, the people within behaving rather like a family, with the GPs behaving like the father and staff within finding their own family role.

Who, within your practice is seen as:

- the father
- the mother
- the naughty child
- the good girl/boy
- the teenager
- the young adult
- the critical parent
- the nurturing parent?

How does this dynamic prevent the practice from developing?

Think how the people in your practice differ from each other in terms of:

- attitudes
- values
- beliefs
- culture.

People demonstrate a whole range of intellectual abilities, not all of which are commonly recognised and developed in the workplace. Scientists in particular often only recognise and give credence to left brain factors such as verbal and mathematical skills. Amongst your colleagues you will find the range of talents: musical ability, interpersonal communication skills, self-knowledge skills, spatial ability, sports achievements, artistic and creative abilities. A good manager will recognise the value of all these skills in those they manage.

According to Freudian psychoanalytic theory, personality is influenced by early experiences (social, family and cultural) as well as adult experiences.[8] In childhood, we all develop 'defences' that help us deal with childhood traumas, and these emerge later in adulthood when we are faced with difficult or stressful situations. Managers have to be aware how people they manage defend themselves when they do not want to be confronted with the difficult feelings again.

Some common defence mechanisms

- Regression – adopting childish patterns of behaviour.
- Fixation – rigid and inflexible behaviour or attitudes.
- Rationalisation – 'covering up' of emotions with intellectual talk.
- Projection – attributing to others the feelings and motives we feel ourselves.

Stress

Some of the most common forms of stress at work have been identified by Cooper *et al.*[9]

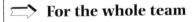 **For the whole team**

Mark the stresses that impact on you and others in your organisation.

- Intrinsic to the job – working conditions.
- Role in the organisation – underload or overload.

- Relationships at work – especially with the boss.
- Career development – especially mid-life.
- Organisational structure and climate – rules and regulations.
- Home–work interface – especially the growth of dual career families.

Who in your practice demonstrates the following personality traits? Remember, these can be perceived as both strengths and weaknesses:

- practical
- serious
- casual
- logical
- analytical
- dependable
- outspoken
- resourceful
- principled
- tolerant
- enthusiastic
- considerate
- detailed
- unstable.

Motivation

A person's motivation, job satisfaction and performance at work will be determined by economic rewards, social relationships, personal attitudes and values, the nature of the work, leadership styles and the satisfaction of the work itself.

In our practice survey we asked about motivations and core values. People need to be asked what motivates them at work. Most of us make judgements about human nature.

 For the whole team

What assumptions do you hold?

- Most people are lazy and dislike work.
- For most people work is as natural as play or rest.
- People must be encouraged or punished if we are to achieve our organisational objectives.
- People like to exercise self-direction and control.

- People like to be committed to work.
- The average person avoids responsibility and prefers to be directed.
- We all like security.
- People accept responsibility readily.
- People work for money only.
- People work to achieve self-esteem and self-actualisation.[10]

The fact is, people are different. We often assume that responsibility, good pay and stimulation are key to people enjoying work. However, this may not be the case. Bear in mind all employees have an interest in work beyond the actual mechanics of the task in hand.

If staff are asked to rank possible motivating factors in order of importance, managers will see that some staff do not want responsibility but direction; some are happy with less pay and less responsibility. Some people come to work because, primarily, they enjoy the team approach and socialising. The following issues can be addressed when analysing staff performance:

- does the practice meet the staff's motivational needs?
- are these taken into account when managing pay and reward systems?

In recruiting, practice managers tend to seek people who are goal oriented, consistent and enjoy taking initiative. It may be appropriate to consider these factors for a senior position, but they would not be applicable to all jobs. However, as we have seen, there is room for increased motivation and decreased apathy through the workforce through introducing a more devolved management style. Through quality circles there is more opportunity for encouraging an increase in personal responsibility and initiative and improving communication between employee and employer.

Once we know more about what motivates people at work, practices can then structure their reward systems accordingly.

 For the partners and manager

Questions to ask yourself

- What do you want to reward?
- How will this support your practice aims and values?
- What are the most important external factors for you?
- What types of reward are possible, practical and affordable?

Here are some possible answers. What do you want to reward?

- Initiative.
- Skills.
- Performance.
- Responsibility.
- Outcomes.
- Good attitudes.
- Professionalism.
- Experience.
- Expertise.

How will this support your practice aims and values?

- Quality service.
- Supports culture.
- Supports change and progress.
- Increases profitability.
- Good response to external pressures.

What are the most important external factors for you?

- Funding.
- Compliance with government rules.
- Patients.

What types of rewards are possible, practical and affordable?

- Training.
- Flexible working days.
- Study leave.
- Public recognition.
- Instant verbal praise.
- Written notes.
- Staff announcements.
- Making requested changes.

In your business plan, include a section on how the practice meets the staff's needs for recognition, intellectual stimulation and socialisation.

For an example template, *see* the website.

If the organisation does not meet people's motivational needs, they become frustrated, and may become aggressive, abusive, short-tempered or feel powerless in their work.

⇨ **For the manager**

How many of the symptoms mentioned above are found in your organisation? Make a note here of five ways you have learned that these behaviours can be reduced.

Control

Research suggests that the manner and amount of control that is exercised in an organisation has an effect on employee performance.[11] Any management system that controls must take into account individual, social and organisational factors which determine people's psychology. Leaders need to be aware of the forces in the manager, in the people they manage, the situation being managed, and the pressures of time.

- Control provides either a safe or a constraining boundary.
- It either restricts or gives freedom of choice.
- It implies something about the individual's standing within the organisation.
- People feel good and powerful when they exercise control.
- The exercise of control helps individuals identify with their workplace.
- People who exercise control may be more willing to conform.

However, there will always be resistance to control from those people with low self-esteem and less belief in authority.

Staff as a resource

Staff are your most valuable asset and are also the most expensive.
  Does the practice:

- flex pay to reflect local factors such as labour and housing costs?
- employ staff who are multi-skilled to increase flexibility in the workplace?
- support existing staff with effective training and redeployment?

Creative organisations are moving away from traditional skill mix by looking at people without professional qualifications but with the relevant skills for the job.

Pay

Many modern organisations are moving away from traditional salaries with automatic incremental pay rises, towards a single spine pay scale, with rewards for job developments, responsibilities and initiative rather than age and seniority. This seems to be having the effect of bringing about a set of relationships that are much more mutually independent than in the past, from a confrontational approach to one of mutual co-operation. A more open relationship then builds, where individuals are more autonomous and less dependent on their organisation.

Performance related pay can have a part to play in large organisations, but is thought to be demotivating and unfair when there are only a handful of people in smaller organisations who would benefit. Any intrinsic (value based non-pay awards) are best demonstrated through allowing individuals to use their creativity and control, allowing them to build their own jobs (job enrichment) and recognising each individual orientation to work.

Extrinsic rewards, measured more formally, can be shown in additional holiday for long term service, training etc. Consider offering flexible pay enhancements. Practices could develop initiatives outside the constraints of the common pay scales, based on identified service needs and reflecting the local position.

Flexible pay enhancements

- Long service awards.
- Childcare arrangements.
- Accelerated access to counselling.
- Accelerated access to medical services.
- Staff achievement awards.
- Job shares.
- Flexible working
    - part time
    - term time only
    - annual hours contracts
    - evening/weekend work
    - home working.

For an example of a pay and rewards strategy, *see* the website.

Other non-pay schemes can be offered.

- Job enlargements which increase the scope and range of tasks.
- Job rotations which decrease boredom and increase variety.
- Job enrichments which:
  - permit workers greater autonomy and freedom
  - allow them to complete a full cycle of the task
  - give them tasks which challenge their abilities
  - change the timing, sequence or pace of the task
  - provide feedback on performance
  - provide them with responsibility for outcomes.

References

1 Department of Health (2000) *The NHS Plan*. DoH, London.

2 Brayfield C (2000) Dodgy business practice. *The Times*, 26 June.

3 Mintzberg H (1973) *The Nature of Managerial Work*. Harper and Row, New York.

4 Clark C and Pratt S (1985) Leadership's four part progress. *Management Today*. **March**. 84–6.

5 Peters TJ and Waterman RH (1982) *In Search of Excellence*. Harper and Row, London.

6 Carlisle J and Parker R (1990) *Beyond Negotiation: redeeming customer–supplier relationships*. Wiley, Chichester.

7 Rogers C (1967) *On Becoming a Person*. Constable, London.

8 Freud S (1973 edition) *New Introductory Lectures on Psychoanalysis*. Penguin, London.

9 Cooper C, Cooper R and Eaker L (1988) *Living with Stress*. Penguin, London.

10 McGregor D (1987) *The Human Side of Enterprise*. Penguin, London.

11 Tannenbaum R and Schmidt WH (1973) How to choose a leadership pattern. *Harvard Business Review*. **May/June**.

Further reading

Bailey A (1997) *Talk Works*. British Communications Ltd, London.

Baker N (2000) *Employment in Focus Briefing No. 20*. Croner, Kingston-upon-Thames.

Bond T (1986) *Games for Social and Life Skills*. Hutchinson, London.

Bor R and McCann D (eds) (1999) *The Practice of Counselling in Primary Care*. Sage Publications, London.

Gardener H (1993) *Frames of Mind* (2e). Fontana, London.

Handy C (1985) *Understanding Organisations.* Penguin, Harmondsworth.

Hertzberg F (1974) *Work and the Nature of Man.* Granada Publishing, London.

Hunt J (1992) *Managing People at Work: a manager's guide to behaviour in organisations* (3e). McGraw-Hill, London.

Maslow A (1987) *Motivation and Personality* (3e). Harper and Row, London.

Mullins LJ (1999) *Management and Organisational Behaviour* (5e). Pitman, London.

Newton J *et al.* (1996) Human resource management in general practice: survey of current practice. *British Journal of General Practice.* **February**.

Weightman J (1993) *Managing Human Resources.* Institute of Personnel and Development, London.

CHAPTER 15

The learning organisation

Training and professional development

'In the NHS we are constantly re-inventing training. Although managers pay it lip-service, they do not often build in budgets for continuing education. It is always a necessary component to ensure that staff of all kinds are properly equipped.'

A Wall[1]

There will be a section in the business plan that looks at training and professional development, and whether the practice has considered the impact of this need. Practices must ensure staff are properly equipped for the job they have been hired to do. Many practice staff do not have the backing of professional bodies to guide and inform their practice as a matter of course, although this will change under the new NHS Act 1999, as we have seen.

- A new body is to be established (the Medical Education Standards Board) which is to provide a coherent, robust and accountable approach to post-graduate medical education.
- A new Leadership Centre will be set up to widen access to workplace development programmes and provide tailored support for potential clinical or managerial leaders.
- Practices will be expected to provide a multi-disciplinary training and development plan as part of the core practice PDP.

The GPs and nurses within the practice almost always meet their professional training obligations, but the practice needs to plan for, encourage and support ancillary staff training, both financially and strategically, at all levels within the organisation. The process needs adapting where appropriate to meet the needs of individuals, not just the organisation.

Does your practice recognise that regular access to paid training will considerably reduce risks:

- ○ of failure
- ○ of complaints
- ○ of disorganisation?

The staff need to feel the weight of an organisation behind them that is willing to invest in and believe in them. The practice should recognise that good training develops and changes people, and encourages personal development.
Further benefits to the organisation:

- resource bids and sponsorship more likely to be accepted
- prompts higher standards of care, effectiveness and efficiency
- reduces organisational and clinical error
- increases staff motivation
- reduces costs associated with poor staff morale and errors.

An organisation that did little training and development would have far greater difficulty in convincing employees (and an industrial tribunal) of the seriousness of its commitment. An organisation would be vulnerable if an employee was sacked or redeployed inappropriately without training. In order to reduce the practice's vulnerability, consider widening the training options to include wider, non-operational issues: equal opportunities, discriminatory practice, quality issues, assertiveness training, counselling skills, group dynamics, time management or team building.

 For the manager

When looking at training and developing staff, do you:

- ○ regularly identify training needs at appraisals
- ○ use appraisals to set objectives and monitor progress
- ○ adapt training where appropriate to meet the needs of individuals, not just the organisation
- ○ improve the level of supervision and support available to staff
- ○ build in budgets for continuing education
- ○ have a training policy that covers everyone in the organisation?

Why have a training policy?

A simple training policy that ensures staff are offered easy and regular access to paid training will considerably reduce the risk of failure, complaints and disorganisation. A training policy shows an organisation is modern, organised and capable: it demonstrates that they have considered and managed risk, and thus is one route of effective defence against litigation.

The training policy

Pro-active organisations have training policies. If the practice wishes to develop in this way it needs to develop a training policy that is explicit, included in the staff induction pack and circulated widely throughout the organisation. The following points need to be addressed.

- Training expectations should be written into job descriptions and should be a contractual obligation, e.g. 'Staff are required to attend at least one training day per year, paid for by the practice. Time off in lieu will be given where appropriate, e.g. if training occurs at the weekend.'
- Consider widening the training options to include wider, non-operational issues: equal opportunities, discriminatory practice, quality issues, assertiveness training, counselling skills, group dynamics, time management and team building.
- Training should be adequately funded and a significant percentage of the staff budget set aside for training.
- All requests for training must be taken seriously.
- If staff bring training demands to you that you consider unrelated to the practice needs, consider asking them to make a presentation, making a case of need and outlining the benefits to the organisation.

The importance of training in any organisation cannot be underestimated, but it is particularly important in health, where, unlike the rest of the public sector, staff training can be haphazard at best, and absent at worst (in local government, for example, training policies are in place and training itself is properly funded and systematic). It is of course easier for larger, more bureaucratic organisations to have organised and astute personnel departments; and it is more likely that training for ancillary or support staff features highly on their agenda.

 In primary care, training is sometimes seen as a waste of resource, and training policies are sadly lacking.

Clinical training is planned for and supported nationally. GPs are now required to keep records of their ongoing clinical development in Personal Development Plans. Other clinical support services, e.g. professions complementary to medicine, physiotherapy or chiropody, have revalidation or registration requirements that ensure they are kept up to date professionally.

However, support or ancillary staff (receptionists, team clerks, administrators and even managers) do not currently have the backing of professional bodies to guide and inform their practice, and so are dependent on their employers, who may or may not invest in their staff in this way

The NHS needs to take a massive leap in its corporate thinking and plan for, encourage and support ancillary staff training, both financially and strategically, at all levels in the organisation, from the GP receptionist through to administrative support teams and managers. A cultural shift is needed.

 ## For the partners and manager

Training can be both formal and ongoing. Consider the following training schedules. Who would need to be involved, by when and what would the cost be?

- Computer training for health visitors.
- Data input to meet medical audit needs.
- Research into evidenced-based nursing.
- Improvement in complaints management.
- Clinical supervision.
- Improving access to clinical records.

For the whole team

Is your training policy:

- proactive?
- known about?
- included in the staff induction pack?
- circulated widely throughout the organisation?

Is:

- training written into job descriptions?
- training a contractual obligation?
- time off in lieu given?
- training adequately funded?
- training taken seriously?

Learning in the practice

A learning organisation continually transforms itself. New and expansive thinking happens, creativity is encouraged and results occur. A practice wishing to develop in any way must encourage and develop their staff by viewing them as stakeholders, customers and partners in the process.

Learning styles

Managers need to consider some of the different motivations and styles of learning amongst their staff. In my practice, I introduced an appraisal system which used open-ended questions. People were invited to write a short paragraph on their views of their work. During a discussion on this appraisal cycle, I was asked if a less formal approach could be used. The feedback given was that the staff were intimidated by the language and 'having to write too much'. The following year we successfully tried out checklists with yes/no answers to performance criteria.

⟹ **For the whole team**

○ Can you prove your practice supports each individual's development?
○ If not, how can you best learn to?

Note some obstacles to learning:

- lack of funding
- lack of understanding and unwillingness to learn about difference
- fearing research and development
- time
- fear of change.

Has your practice got what it takes to learn in the new NHS?

○ What are your practice learning priorities?
○ Do you know where to get the information you need?

What are your learning and training needs? Write your own learning plan. This requires an honest and valuable analysis of your present position and how that position was reached. Identify the progress required, and analyse what must be achieved to obtain that progress.

○ Where have you been?
○ Where are you now with regard to current knowledge, abilities and opportunities?

○   Where do you want to get to with regard to job/career and life goals?
○   How will you get there?
○   How will you know when you've arrived? (Goals are sharpened when the learner has to say how the learning will be measured.)

Developing practices will be interested in adopting new, more modern training and development methods. For good learning to occur it has to be an active process. The learner constructs their own learning and therefore actively participates in the process. Learning then is more complete, and more likely to fix. The teacher's role here is to facilitate or mentor, not to impart knowledge. New learning is about empowering the individual.

That said, we all have a preferred learning style, and for some people the older style of passive absorption suits. Researchers have classified certain types of learner:

- the activist who learns by doing
- the pragmatist who learns best when the practical application is obvious
- the theorist who needs to understand the fundamental principles
- the reflector who learns by thinking about things.[2]

In general practice, the traditional available learning routes only suited the theorist or reflector. There are however, other, different ways of learning that can be beneficial and broaden management and people skills in particular. There are ways of learning that can be inspirational and fun, and can further personal development. These methods may suit the pragmatist or activist better.

⟹ **For the partners and manager**

An effective manager understands group process and behaviour, as then they can get the best out of their staff. For this, they may need to look beyond their traditional learning routes to meet new government expectations. They will need to demonstrate they are broadening and developing their staff. Self-managed learning is one way of meeting this need, and builds on the concept of team and group training.

What is self-managed learning?

Basically, it is where a group of colleagues who share a common purpose meet to:

- share problems and ideas
- reflect on ways of managing difficult or new situations.

Learning sets are one way self-managed learning can occur. Practice managers and doctors benefit hugely from this sort of learning.

In self-managed learning, each participant is given equal time within the group. The person receiving the focus of attention learns, and evaluates, for themselves. There is a shift in his or her ideas in relation to the issue. The process can be supportive yet challenging and empowering, as each person takes personal responsibility for their own learning. Many PCTs are supporting the development of learning sets and self-managed learning.

However, managers need to be aware that some people find self-learning difficult.

- They feel that others should be responsible for their development.
- They are unable to work successfully as part of a group.
- They believe they have nothing to learn about anything.

 For the partners and manager

Sell the advantages of self-learning to the practice, and write up your reasons for promoting it in your business plan. You are demonstrating you are a learning organisation that is open to change.

Some advantages to self-learning

- More innovative solutions to problems emerge.
- Learning is disseminated more widely.
- The organisation as a whole often develops a learning approach to problem solving.
- Networking benefits: participants find other people who they can rely on to continue to support them through change.
- Participants learn to support and challenge behaviour appropriately. They actively listen, are honest and open; and they take these skills back to their organisations.
- The facilitation skills can be learned and extended to others.
- Progress may be made on problems to which there may have been no clear solutions before.
- Effort and resources are not wasted on inappropriate learning.
- Participants are more open to further self-development.
- The focus is on approaching and dealing with practical problems, not on theory.
- Risk is soon regarded as a developmental and acceptable tool.
- People adapt the process to suit their own needs.

- Real issues are addressed, there is practical and immediate application of the learning.
- Individuals identify their own needs and arrive at their own solutions.

Application in practice: teams and groups

One of the biggest advantages of self-managed learning is that it is an aid to improve and develop team working in general practice, as it is an organisation small enough to be able to organise itself in this way. The premise is to influence and assist change by offering support for change to occur from within, through empowering individuals and assisting them with the transition. It is a particularly useful approach when an organisation needs to undergo a large cultural change: to become one that is more responsive to patients' needs, for example. To set this up, the whole practice has to be committed to a new way of working: this is ongoing training and needs emotional and practical investment from everyone in the organisation.

The principles of self-managed learning can easily be applied to a general practice team if the practice apply what they learn from their business planning process, problem solve, and manage the changes required in the practice.

The principles:

- practices need to begin to work collectively at problems and problem solving – reversing a top driven culture
- practices need to spend time acknowledging the history of organising things in a certain way
- no change will occur without the very central involvement of the main stakeholders: the GPs.

Partners must avoid interfering in operational (day to day) management decisions and actions made by the team. Thus the GPs learn to trust, and the staff can see their own ideas and initiatives taking shape.

Learn about groups

Effective group working takes skill to develop. Those within the group need to learn some of the rules of group dynamics:

- a group leader will emerge if unelected
- keep the group as small as possible – in a group of eight people, there are eight different agendas and potentially 28 different relationships going on
- be aware of non-verbal behaviour
- be aware of the tendency for men to interrupt women or dominate the space
- be aware that oppression rules: the 'experts' and higher social classes will dominate

- be sensitive to quieter members and give them space
- allow the leader to make mistakes.[3]

Different personality types are found within groups and each needs to be skilfully managed:[4]

Personality type	Plus points	Potential difficulties

Completer–finisher.	Likes detail.
	Will complete a task.
	Can concentrate.
	Good judgement skills.
	Meets deadlines.
	High standards.
	Very accurate.
		Can be pedantic.
		Poor tolerance of casual
		  or flippant behaviour.
		Can be over anxious or
		  introvert.

Implementor.	Practical. Systematic. Disciplined. Loyal. Reliable. Efficient.	Can be rigid.

Monitor–evaluator.	Able to analyse problems,
	  ideas and options.
	
	Good judgement skills.
		Serious minded and cautious,
		  which upsets the casual
		  worker.
		Slow thinker.
		Can be critical.

Specialist.	High professional standards. Expert in narrow field. In-depth knowledge and experience.	Not broad minded. Lacks interest in other subjects.
Team worker.	Mild. Sociable. Supportive and concerned about others. Diplomatic, flexible and adaptable. Sensitive and perceptive to needs of team. Good listener. Popular. Good at raising morale, reducing conflict and promoting co-operation.	Can be indecisive.

Resource investigator.	Enthusiastic, extrovert, relaxed and
	  inquisitive.
	Good communicator and negotiator.
	Can think on their feet.
	Develops others' ideas.
	Investigates contacts and resources.
		Needs constant stimulation
		  of others.

Shaper.	Single minded, extrovert with
	  strong drive.
	Thrives under pressure.
	Achiever.
	Good at overcoming obstacles.
	Prepared to take unpopular decisions.
		Competitive, aggressive and
		  challenging.
		Pushy.
		Can be frustrated.
		May lack understanding
		  of others.

Plant.	Creative innovator. Good at generating new ideas. Can solve complex problems.	Unorthodox. Impractical. Poor communicator. Sensitive to praise or criticism.

Make a note of the personality types in your team. Note how groups develop. Tuckman noted that groups pass through different stages in their development, they evolve over time.[5]

Task	Activity	Features
Forming.	Define the nature and boundaries of task.	Grumbling or moaning about task. Behaviour meandering and ineffective.
Storming.	Questioning the value of exercise.	Challenging behaviour. Opposition. Defensive behaviour.
Norming.	Opening up and inviting.	Expressing feelings. Defining tasks. Mutually supportive.
Performing.	Effectively pursuing the task.	Interpersonal issues now disregarded. Achieving.
Ending.	Facing the loss of the group experience.	By denial – we'll meet again. By bargaining – task not yet complete. With anger – nobody appreciates us.

Note how people within your practice behave in groups. Discuss these behaviours within your group and ask them to seek out ways of reinforcing positive behaviour and challenging negative behaviour. For example, who:

- takes initiative
- takes leadership
- offers directions
- seeks suggestions
- calms things down
- encourages compromises
- notes down the minutes
- is obstructive or negative
- keeps time
- challenges appropriately
- generates ideas
- criticises
- offers irrelevant ideas?

See the website for some more best practice ideas on meetings and groups.

Where a practice has adopted a self-managed learning style, a culture that respects change is born:

- staff feel respected and empowered
- the practice culture may shift from one where staff are passive and dependent and resentful of change, to one where they are more confident and innovative
- organisation is clearer, roles and responsibilities are centrally understood and defined
- there is more control and potential for growth
- results happen and decisions are made collectively, not autocratically or through independent management action
- there is better communication, leading to everyone understanding each other's working patterns and recognising others' stresses
- there is anticipation of harmonisation of working practice amongst doctors.

This kind of culture adapts well to change. Because the change operates from within, and is not top led, it is cultivated rather than managed. There will be an attitude of growth, of learning not instruction or control. People will know their ideas and values are listened to and respected. The management style moves from a limiting task-centred approach (with the main objective to get the task done) towards a people-centred approach. Part of managing change (and people) is recognising change can only be managed, not imposed. Expect the central management structure and processes within the practice to change completely, and the business to develop as a result.

References

1   Wall A (1999) *Health Service Journal.* 7 January.

2   Honey P and Mumford A (1986) *The Manual of Learning Styles.* Honey Publications, Maidenhead.

3   Middleton J (2000) *The Team Guide to Communication.* Radcliffe Medical Press, Oxford.

4   Belbin RM (1991) *Management Teams: why they succeed or fail.* Heinemann, London.

5   Tuckman B (1965) Development sequences in small groups. *Psychological Bulletin.* **63**: 384–99.

CHAPTER 16

Preparing for the future

'If you can keep your head when all about you are losing theirs, then you just don't understand the nature of the mess we're in.'

Tony Turrill[1]

Organisations operate within an increasingly volatile environment and are in a state of constant change. Change is an inescapable part of our working lives, and yet, as we have seen, most people resist change. It is very important, therefore, for managers to adopt a clear strategy for managing change, so that new ideas and innovations are not seen as threatening to the practice. This last chapter looks at:

- what change is and what it means to people
- some of the ways managers can overcome the resistance to change
- how to manage change
- how to set goals.

The chapter ends by looking at some of the ways practice managers can expect to be working in the future.

Managing change

Change is a constant in the workplace and world. To survive and grow organisations must adjust to change, and be alert to the need for it. Change is also messy. Just when you think you have arrived you find you have hardly begun. Why change?

Which of these do you agree with?

- Change is the key to progress.
- We can choose not to change.
- Change affects every organisation.

- Change is always imposed.
- Managing change can make all the difference.
- Change is very risky behaviour.
- People react differently to change.
- Change can be unsettling.

Change can feel like all of these things, yet we cannot now escape it – if we assume no change in the way the NHS is run, the choices will be harsher. Some innovative, well managed organisations have fought to adapt to a turbulent world.

The less sensitive and proactive are lost. We are moving, globally and organisationally:[2]

From	To
An industrial society	An information society
Forced technology	User-friendly technology
National economy	World economy
Long term	Short term
Centralisation	Decentralisation
Institutional help	Self-help
Representative democracy	Participative democracy
Hierarchies	Networking
Either/or	Multiple options

We have already seen some changes operating in our own careers. Jobs are no longer for life, we need to allow individuals to join and leave an organisation at several points in their career. There is a movement from boss–subordinate relationship towards procedures which encourage staff to work in flexible groups of equals. Work is no longer permanent and long term, and reward is more closely allied to achievement.

Change has to be managed, and as with any management process it needs to be understood before it can be managed. We need to understand:

- how to plan for change
- how to implement change
- how to evaluate change.

Within this, we need to identify:

- the core purpose of the organisation
- the future that we desire
- some of the forces driving change
- the need for change
- our own reactions to change
- some of the resistance to change
- the size and shape of the work to be done

- the cost of the work
- how to establish a climate which enables the work to take place.

Practices and their practice managers must prepare themselves personally and professionally for changes ahead. Throughout the book, it has been made clear that GPs and managers need to look at their personal development (management roles, leadership styles, time management and goal setting) as well as project management (business planning and building a team) to be better equipped to face the future. For GPs, one of the biggest challenges is learning to look more broadly and strategically at events. There is a debate about whether medicine is a science or an art. A science such as medicine uses traditionally the reductionist theory, where the item under scrutiny is dissected and analysed in smaller and smaller units until it is understood. A broad sweep or artistic approach would look more holistically at an event. 'Soft' scientific theory such as psychology, or organisational analysis, is therefore often hard for doctors.

 Doctors need to learn to adapt to a more holistic way of working, and take a broader view of their organisation.

Change is fundamental to progress. It is, in the present political climate, necessary for survival. Practices are facing some big challenges. With yet another re-organisation on our hands with the transition from PCGs to PCTs, managers are looking at enormous changes in their own careers, their management style and job brief. Practices have already been participating in major organisational change as they prepare to become small businesses operating within a consortium instead of in isolation. In management change is traditionally seen as common, rapid and huge in its effects; the public sector is no longer exempt.

The changing role of the practice manager

Practice managers have had to adapt and learn fast. Their own careers are reshaping: they are taking on additional responsibilities and they are learning to delegate the administrative tasks that previously formed the main bulk of their workload. They are looking instead at needs analysis, business plans, forecasting, projecting and negotiating. Their managing is changing in both style and content. As more responsibility is taken on, a different kind of respect is demanded which has both financial and personal implications. Practice managers unused to this new role may need to learn new personal skills to support their new sense of self – assertion and negotiating skills, for example.

Managers now need to persuade their employers that their time must no longer be taken up with direct administration, but be allocated for planning and monitoring. Good management is proactive rather than reactive, so it is anticipated that those practices which succeed will be those that have actively prepared for change. Change is unsuccessful when it has been improvised and forced rather than planned.

To develop, managers need to:

- be experimental and flexible
- keep informed of developments within the profession
- monitor medical trends
- assess changes and developments in attitudes and behaviour of competitors and patients
- accept medicine can no longer afford to be complacent regarding its relationship with the consumer.

The changing role of the practice

It is not only the manager and the perceptions of their role which need to change. No member of staff is exempt and good communication will be increasingly important.

- Staff will need to be kept informed and abreast of changes in policy and workload.
- New ideas must be regularly discussed and information shared.
- New techniques must be tried out where appropriate.
- Staff should be encouraged to raise issues affecting their work.
- Staff must indicate as soon as possible if accepted practice is inappropriate.
- Innovation and adaptability must become part of everyday life.

Why is change so problematic? Change always presents dilemmas, the need to:

- exercise judgement without sacrificing principles – if you have a fundamental belief in the value of people and respect for their individuality, how do you square that with making ten of them redundant?
- experiment versus the need to be right
- manage the present versus manage the change
- manage uncertainty versus certainty
- balance necessary bureaucracy versus innovation
- focus on external changes versus internal changes.

There are no simple answers. Balances need to be struck, without compromising principles.

Managers need to understand that resistance to change is often the expression of insecurity and fear, as it exposes people to uncertainty and may alter work patterns for the worse. It is therefore more acceptable when the objectives and application are understood and do not offer a threat to security. The practice vision will alter; many staff, especially long term ones, resent change. The managers need to persuade their staff that change is neither difficult nor unnecessary. John Harvey Jones, Chairman of ICI, encapsulated this when he said: 'the problem is not to get the ship (ICI) moving in the right direction, but to get it moving at all!'

What individual resistance to change do we know about?

Resistance is found at both the personal and organisational level.

- Habit – established customs and practice.
- Personal inconvenience.
- Own (biased) view of situation.
- Loss of own freedom.
- Cost of change.
- Past contracts and agreements.
- Threat to power.
- Financial implications.
- Fear of the unknown.
- Security bedded in the past.

 **For the whole team**

What are your own reasons not to change?

- We don't have the time or money.
- We tried it five years ago and it didn't work.
- Everyone will blame me if it doesn't work.
- It's not in our plan.
- We need evolution not revolution.
- Why fix it if it isn't broken?

How do you react to change?

Do you feel confident, excited or uncertain and frightened?

Identify the need for change

- Stay alert to the need for change.
- Consider where you are now.
- Consider where you want to be.

Plan for change

'*Let's find out what everyone is doing and then stop them from doing it.*'

AP Herbert

Effective change needs careful planning. Identify who the change will affect, consult your team, and map your environment:

- identify who needs to be involved
- identify who will be opposed and therefore not assist
- identify who will not oppose but still not assist
- identify who will support if someone else leads
- identify who will want it to happen, and make it happen
- recognise where there is agreement and conflict
- examine training needs
- allocate responsibilities
- look at the opposing forces (what pushes and what restrains).

One way to see these more clearly is by constructing a *forcefield analysis*, where you examine the driving and restraining forces in order that they may be managed more effectively, e.g.:

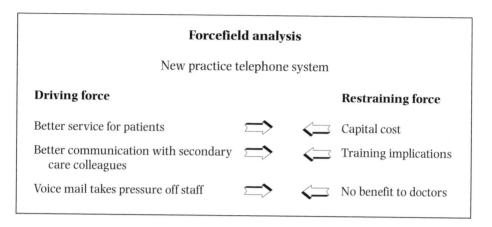

Forcefield analysis

New practice telephone system

Driving force			Restraining force
Better service for patients			Capital cost
Better communication with secondary care colleagues			Training implications
Voice mail takes pressure off staff			No benefit to doctors

For some other ideas on implementing change and change management, *see* the website. *See* the website for an example case study of how one practice applied change within their team.

How to make change successful

'If change were logical, a linear process, there would not be a problem. But the strategy setting and planning processes take time, induce suspicion in those not involved, and generate a workload that feels overwhelming.'

Tony Turrill[1]

Visionary leadership assists by setting an entrepreneurial climate which legitimises experimentation. There is no short cut, no substitute, for involving people in order to generate their commitment.

- If the practice vision is dynamic, staff will be used to change being introduced.
- Change is successful where it has been preceded by other successful changes.
- The people who are to be affected by the change help shape and implement it.
- Those affected take some share of the benefits.
- There is a clear set of cultural beliefs.
- There is a free flow of information across the organisation.
- Practices with known group leaders (who may or may not be the manager) will be the winners.

- Those managing the change must have the energy, confidence and commitment to carry it through.
- Newly appointed managers have an advantage.
- New staff find change easier.
- Democratic, consistent and fair leadership styles are important.

Successful change programmes are complex and bitty and contain a number of ingredients. Change is organic and dynamic. It involves:

- innovation
- ice-breaking
- leadership
- vision
- strategy
- drivers.

Here are some pointers to assist you in managing the change process. Think about how you implement change in your practice and see if you match up.

- Allow for a period of transition.
- Know who your stakeholders are.
- Seek commitment.
- Secure role model acceptance of change.
- Problem solve collectively.
- Break things into steps: what needs to be done, when and by whom.
- Monitor.
- Explain.
- Share the vision.
- Share the fundamental beliefs.
- Be honest.
- Encourage.
- Listen to and understand the negatives.
- Delegate responsibilities.
- Find a critical mass of support(ers).
- Eliminate unnecessary bureaucracy.
- Establish learning systems linked to change.

Be aware of the effects on your staff of too much stress, and the effects of speedy change:

Shock → defensive withdrawal → acknowledgement → adaptation

Allow for, and accommodate these feelings, and respond to them by offering support, self-awareness/development training programmes and counselling if necessary.

Monitor and evaluate

Did the change accomplish what it set out to do? Should the change be abandoned or adjusted? Talk to your team and find out. Work on continuous improvement.

Those dependent on the organisation should not notice the change if routine work is under control so there is time to innovate and implement the new ways of working. It has been said that managers must view change and innovation as opportunities to seize rather than as threats to fear. We will only learn to master change when we encourage, welcome and incorporate it into our personal and professional lifestyle. The benefits of change can be positive (greater creativity) with better performance and increased achievement. Even the mistakes can be instructive. Change can create situations where the manager's own talents can shine and be rewarded.

Goal setting

Before practices can achieve any change, goals have to be set. Goals tell us where we want to go. Objectives tell us how to get there.

What is it that prevents practices from achieving their goals?

Most practices aim to provide a fast, flexible and friendly service to their patients. They aim for an evidence-based and accountable approach to the delivery of care. Most try to ensure practice resources are targeted appropriately. GPs generally aim to be professional, respectful, honest, considerate and courteous. However, some practices hope to do all this without any management involvement at all! The GPs think if they are friendly and committed, this is enough. They work hard but forget that the above can only happen with good organisation and planning ahead. As most GPs work reactively, much of what goes on in general practice happens almost by chance; big changes are rarely planned.

Operationally, almost all practice systems are now risk assessed and practices are getting better at managing risk. However, in order to minimise risk most practices need to address the major strategic issues and not simply concentrate on the operational management issues.

 Practices need to check out the health of their organisation, and map their environment.

 Practices need to agree the core purpose of their business.

 Practices need to paint a vision of their future.

Not all visions will be compatible. There needs to be agreement within the partnership to define mutually acceptable aims. Here we look at some of the common problems in general practice that prevent them from changing and developing.

 Practices need to share their priorities.

So often in general practice ideas and plans are thought up in isolation – if you are lucky, by all partners, or one partner and the practice manager; rarely the whole practice. More often than not the idea takes hold and suddenly, with no discussion, the staff are informed there is to be an extra clinic, or the lunchtime session moved to early afternoon, or a new telephone system is to be bought.

Change is difficult to manage at the best of times, but unless everyone is part of this type of discussion, sabotage is common and the plan will fail.

 Practices need to find out the level of commitment, and allocate the responsibilities fairly.

If someone in the practice tries out the new idea, and it succeeds, and especially if it costs, the PCG/T is approached for money. Rarely are the ideas talked through with interested stakeholders first. Sharing the plan first with external lead professionals helps clarify some of the wider issues, and firms up the proposals so that everyone involved can see whether any new plans are going to be viable or not.

 Practices rarely manage conflict well.

GPs tend to shy away from managing conflict. A healthy organisation openly discusses conflict, and accepts that conflict is a normal, and inevitable, reality of management and organisational behaviour. Managers and GPs who find conflict difficult need to recognise people's needs, expectations, differences and attributes. If the practice is democratic and open, it accepts that people collectively build and shape an organisation. The process is participative and is based on mutual trust and consideration. If the practice rules are fair and equitable, and personal and organisational goals are met and integrated, workers have a sense of identity and feel valued.

In your business plan, note honestly how conflict is managed.

The practice has been dynamic and developing, and now needs to build on the achievements of the previous years, strengthening the partnership after a rather shaky history and work to build on the fruits of their hard work. There are inevitably outstanding problems carried from the old building, financial commitments, jealousies, fears and threats. These need managing tactfully by the incoming manager, who needs to address any favouritism and develop staff so change is welcomed not feared.

Why do we need goals?

Goals are useful because they:

- provide a standard of performance
- provide a basis for planning and control
- are the basis for objectives and policies in the organisation
- give an indication of what the organisation is like to others
- help develop the commitment of individuals
- reduce uncertainty in decision making
- help to focus direction
- influence the structure of the organisation
- help determine the nature of technology to be applied.[3]

In the first chapter we looked at goal setting. Now it is time to set these down with a step-by-step approach detailing how your practice can achieve their aims.

 For the whole team

How to set goals

Some ideas to help you set goals for the practice:

The creative approach

Explore the problem space.

- How is this a problem?
- When, where, what and/or how specifically does this occur?
- When did it become a problem?
- Why is it important?
- Was there a time when this wasn't a problem? What is different now?
- What solutions have you already applied?

Explore the solution space. Give at least three possible solutions to this problem.

- ○   Which one jumps out at you as being the most feasible?
- ○   For you, what is the solution?
- ○   How will you know when this is solved?
- ○   What would be the first step to making that a reality?
- ○   When and where are you going to take that step?

Spend ten minutes listing all the things you would like to achieve if you had a lifetime in healthcare.

1

2

3

4

5

6

7

8

9

10

List those goals you could reasonably achieve within ten years.

1

2

3

4

5

Make a list of those goals you will achieve this year.

1

2

3

The logical approach

Start by addressing the achievements of the previous year and potential developments for the future. Include any plans the practice has for improvement. You may wish to itemise these under the following headings:

- staff
- clinical
- finance
- premises
- marketing and promotion.

The items can be as large or small as you wish – use them to form a checklist of things done/to do. They could include, for example:

- secretaries to receive training on mail merge – training date booked
- prepare and print a practice charter – manager co-written section 1–3 with Dr X
- reprint practice leaflet – next year
- redecorate treatment room – next year.

What are you currently doing towards meeting your present goal?

1

2

3

4

5

6

What do you plan to do next year?

1

2

3

4

5

6

Now refer back to your picture in Chapter 1 and some of those solutions. Write down any solutions that, in retrospect, you feel would work.

1

2

3

4

5

Write down those that you would not consider.

1

2

3

4

5

Are there any left over you are not sure about? Do not dismiss them. Make a note of them here and come back to them at a later date.

1

2

3

4

5

Write or draw the consequences of some of the solutions you are considering.

Objectives and targets

Here is a selection of the aims one practice set:

- Improve communication.
- Consolidate services.
- Skill up management to work strategically not operationally.
- Use information systems constructively.
- More clinical and managerial delegation.
- GPs to measure their role in taking responsibility for their business.
- Need to improve resource management and develop appropriate management systems.
- Plan ahead financially.

How does this fit into a plan?

Once the practice has identified their priorities, and what they can afford over the next 2–5 years, they then stage the development, marking each target with an aim (what the plan is) and objective (how to map the outcome).

- Detail your targets for the year to come, as summarised in the executive summary.
- Note how success will be measured once the object has been achieved.
- Note who is responsible for achieving it by when, using basic *who, why, what, where* and *when* headings. Note the cost, if any, of your plan, and when you hope to achieve it by.
- Be specific and clear about your objectives.

See the website for some examples.

Collectively discuss how the aims should be prioritised, agree how success will be measured once the object has been achieved, and who is responsible for achieving it by when. With the date, cost and achieved date noted, you have a complete record of the process.

Objectives should be:

- measurable
- realistic and achievable
- timebound.

Note also any critical success factors, and build in a system for monitoring whether or not you have achieved your objectives.

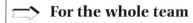 **For the whole team**

See the website for a sample template.

Strategic snapshot

Once the practice is stable they will be in a position to see the long term aspirations they will need to manage. These issues will help to inform the future internal business planning meetings.

Identify any longer term (3–5 year) issues you will need to manage (growth of population etc.) and any resource implications you anticipate.

See the website for an example.

2001 and beyond

What will the GP practice of the future look like?

Healthy practices will be organic – always moving, changing and adapting to circumstances. Individuals will be encouraged to develop initiative. Team working will be accepted. These practices will go part way towards a TQM approach:

- managed through shared vision
- systems designed to liberate
- appropriate involvement and co-operation from employees
- customer led
- emphasis on quality
- focused on long term results
- biased to action.

Another researcher identifies TQM slightly differently. Their view is that the quality organisation:

- involves all operations and management
- is led from the top
- believes the customer is king
- emphasises rational information collection and analysis
- examines the costs of poor quality
- involves people
- believes teamwork is crucially important
- thinks creatively
- plans ahead.[4]

What will the manager of the future do?

- Plan strategically.
- Organise.
- Motivate, develop and feed back.
- Clarify aims and objectives.
- Measure (formally and informally).
- Self-assess.
- Analyse.
- Respond to and manage change.
- Aim for TQM.
- Delegate responsibility.
- Manage:
    - resources
    - people
    - activities
    - information
    - energy
    - quality
    - projects.

For this they will need:

- knowledge
- behavioural skills (assertiveness, communication and influencing skills)
- complex cognitive abilities
- self-knowledge
- emotional resilience
- personal drive.

The practice manager of the future will need to learn how to be truly accountable to their organisations, and more involved in policy formation than at present.

As a result of taking the practice through the business planning process, some of the values and attributes for excellence will be noted. Various researchers have looked at what contributes to excellence in a healthy organisation.[5-7]

Here are some of the factors.

- A bias for action.
- Achieving constant renewal.
- Close to the customer.
- Autonomy and entrepreneurship.
- Hands-on, value driven.
- Simple structure and lean staff.

- Open discussion of conflict.
- Strongly held beliefs.
- Recognises people's needs, expectations, differences and attributes.
- Checks that personal and organisational goals are met and integrated.
- Exploits the organisation.
- Is democratic, participative, just and equitable.
- Develops mutual trust and consideration.
- Has a concern for quality.
- Gives opportunities for personal development.
- Re-shapes culture.
- Drives radical change.
- People have identity and value.
- There is a sense of excitement.
- There is confidence in management.
- Voluntary and personal commitment.
- There is a competitive edge.
- Leadership is developed.
- Makes team working work.

Has your practice any of these qualities already? Can you aspire to this?

References

1   Turrill T (1986) *Change and Innovation*. NHS Management Series No. 10. Institute of Health Service Management, London.

2   Naisutt J (1982) *Megatrends*. Warner, New York.

3   Kast F and Rosenzweig J (1985) *Organisation and Management: a systems and contingency approach* (4e). McGraw-Hill, New York.

4   Pentecost D (1991) Quality management: the human factor. *European Participation Monitor*. **2**: 8–10.

5   Institute of Management (1994) *Management Development to the Millennium*. Institute of Management, London.

6   Heller R (1977) *In Search of European Excellence*. HarperCollins Business, Harlow.

7   Peters T and Waterman R (1992) *In Search of Excellence*. Harper and Row, London.

Further reading

Armson R and Paton R (eds) (1994) *Organisations, Cases, Issues, Concepts*. Open University Press, Oxford.

Additional useful contacts

For doctors

The British Medical Association	www.bma.org.uk	For press releases, circulars etc.
The Department of Health	www.open.gov/doh/outlook.htm	For circulars and current information.
Medline	www.nim.nih.gov	For access to medical journals.
The Health Service Journal	www.hsj.co.uk	For current clinical news.
Health Promotion Department	www.promotinghealth.org	
Cochrane Centre	www.update – software.com/ccweb/cochrane/cdsr/htm	

For patients

What Doctors Don't Tell You	www.wddty.co.uk
For patient leaflets and help	www.patient.co.uk

For managers

The Institute of Healthcare Management	www.ihm.org.uk
Chief Executive Bulletins, circulars and announcements from the DoH	www.doh.gov.uk/cebulletin.htm

Index